W9-CMS-045

# BRONZES
## 1800–1930
## SCULPTORS & FOUNDERS

# BRONZES

## SCULPTORS & FOUNDERS
### 1800-1930

by HAROLD BERMAN

**ABAGE/Publishers**

Chicago, Illinois

# CREDITS

Editor & Production Director
**Dinah Polen**

Graphic Arts Consultant
**Elaine Esch**

Photographic Consultant
**Alice Cobb**

Lithographic Consultant
**Theodore Daniels**

Lithographer
**Bockman Printing, Inc.**

FIRST EDITION

Copyright © 1974 by Harold Berman

Abage Publishers

6430 N. Western Ave., Chicago, Illinois 60645

Library of Congress Catalog Card Number: 74-78612

Printed in the United States of America

*DEDICATED*

*to*

*My Mother and Father*

FLORA
By J. Rennafer
Dated 1891 Painted patina

# CONTENTS

FOREWORD 9

Criteria for
Evaluation of Bronzes 11

**PART ONE**

Bronze Sculptures
Photographic Section 15

Founders and Sculptors 189

**PART TWO**

General References 195

Founders' Seals 196

Identifying Characteristics
of Bronzes and White Metals 200

What is meant by Signed,
Listed, Dated and Numbered 205

Characteristics and
Identification of Patinas 210

Care, Cleaning and
Polishing of Bronzes 213

Applying
Your Own Patina 216

How to Photograph Bronzes 218

INDEX 221

MELODIE
By E. Villanis
France c1900 Gilded patina

# Foreword

*1800 to 1930 were years that produced a multitude of highly gifted sculptors and skilled founders. They left a heritage of never to be duplicated works in bronze. The dominant characteristic of this period was realism—lifelike beauty of face and figure. Sculptor, founder and patineur, as a team, worked tirelessly toward this end.*

*I have selected for presentation in this book a few hundred representative works. Whether signed by a "known" sculptor, or signed at all for that matter, did not enter into my decision. The considerations were: interesting and beautiful subject matter; fine foundry work; availability to collectors; and bronzes not previously photographed for publication.*

*The book's unique format will allow a browser to look at the 129 photo-pages without being distracted by text matter. For those who prefer to delve, descriptive, information capsules appear on 42 special pages. For those who want to acquire more general information, there is a section of practical articles.*

*This book will be especially valuable to collectors and investors who have searched in vain for published materials dealing with available bronzes of this 1800 to 1930 period.*

*All works presented here are from private collections.*

FLOWER FAIRIES
By M. Moreau
Photo Section, Fig. 262.

# Criteria for Evaluation of Bronzes

Collecting bronzes, whether it be for pleasure or profit, can be a challenging and rewarding pastime—especially if one is knowledgeable as to what to buy, what to avoid, and why.

Determining what a bronze is worth is essentially a relative matter. Rarely does one find two pieces identical in every respect. Worth, consequently, must be based on individual judgment, knowledge and experience.

### Lighting and viewing

The initial step before purchasing any bronze is to inspect it thoroughly. It should always be viewed under the brightest possible lighting conditions, as well as from all angles. Inspection of a piece in direct sunlight is most desirable as it reveals the figure at its worst, showing up any flaws that may be present.

The best method for inspecting a statue is to stand in one spot and have the light shine directly on the figure as you swivel it a full 360°. The basic characteristics you should be noting and evaluating are the following:
- METALLIC COMPOSITION. Determine what metal the figure is composed of. Was it cast in bronze or white metal? Does it have a coating of copper over another material, such as chalk, porcelain or pottery? Is it solid cast or hollow?

Do not be confused by the term "solid bronze," which suggests that the entire piece is one solid mass. Though the inside of a figure may be hollow, it may be properly referred to as being "solid bronze" if its metallic composition is bronze.

• FINISH. Examine the statue to decide if it has its original patina. Look into all its corners and deep crevices. If the finish is original, the hidden areas will have the same patina as the outside surfaces; that's because the piece was totally immersed in the patining agents. Today, very fine new patinas are given to bronze figures through the use of spray-cans and other spray apparatus. Although they produce a smooth pleasing finish, they fail to thoroughly reach and cover the deepest crevices. This shortcoming is caused by the very nature of this method of application; that is, airborne materials, when blown into closed areas, build up air-pockets which prevent proper coverage.

A statue should also be examined to determine what type of patina it has. Is it paint, lacquer, varnish, or applied acid? Figures that were finished with acid, look as if they have a natural tarnish or oxidation; in fact, it is common for pieces with such finishes to be mistaken for old bronzes naturally tarnished by age.

Generally, a refinished piece is worth less than one having its original patina. However, a bronze with a fine new finish may have a value equal to, or even more, than one with an original patina in poor condition.

• GOLD BRONZE. Statues touted by sellers as "gold bronzes" require cautious inspection before reaching for the checkbook. A bronze that has been stripped of its patina and then highly polished may look like gold (or brass); however, this does not make it a "gold bronze." Neither is one sprayed or painted gold a "gold bronze" unless you are specifically referring to color.

A true "gold bronze" is one covered with no less than a thin layer of gold, by one of several legitimate methods. It will have a satin-like appearance, not a bright highly polished look. A gold-bronze finish in good condition adds value to a piece; a bronze stripped of its finish and colored gold has a lesser value. Inexpensive gold testing kits may be purchased by those who desire positive proof.

• COMPLEXITY OF THE CAST. More than one major form on a single base is referred to as a "group," which, of course, has more value than a solitary figure. Two figures, though, will not necessarily be worth twice the price of one, nor will three triple the value of the piece.

• MISSING PARTS. When examining complexities of a cast, check all sides of the statue carefully. Look for filled-in holes on both the figures and base; this would be an indication of missing objects. Lead deposits and tiny screw-holes in palms, in particular, tell of missing parts which may, or may not, be of major importance, depending upon whether the object is the focal point or an element essential to the figure's action.

12

• MARBLE BASE. Does a statue have a marble base, or should it have one? Old marble bases were carefully made with ridges and steps, the contour following that of the bronze base, whether it be round, oval, rectangular, octagonal, etc. Not all bronzes were set on these luxurious second bases.

Statues which, by composition and design, were meant to be viewed from all angles usually were fitted with round second bases of bronze or marble. These second bases contained knobs which fit into receptacles anchored in the figure's base. These cup-like receptacles are your clue to a missing second base.

• SIZE. Generally, the larger the statue, the greater its value. Miniatures, on the other hand, are exceptionally desirable and valued, out of proportion to their relative size. Smallness of size tends to enhance the marketability of many pieces.

• DETAIL. Fine detailing increases value. Some fine sculptors, however, employed soft muted detail, which in no way detracted from the figure's beauty or lessened its value. With a little experience, one can learn to distinguish between poor craftsmanship in detailing or intended artistic style.

• UNFINISHED AND RECAST PIECES. Don't overlook the backside of a piece. Fine statues will be beautifully finished in every visible corner, including those on the backside.

Also, note if short-cuts have been taken by fusing and melting elements of the figure together in an attempt to circumvent extra work.

Smothered detail, mold marks, and overly thick fingers and toes are clues that a piece may have been re-cast.

• MISCELLANEOUS FLAWS AND DAMAGE. Beware of crossed eyes, dented noses, repaired fingers, loose appendages, inappropriate facial expression, and clumsy composition. These are items that can affect the value and saleability of a piece.

• IDENTIFICATION MARKS. A signature, founder's seal, number, or any type of special marking increases the value and marketability of a bronze. But, it remains for the individual himself to decide how high a premium he is willing to pay for them.

Many poor-quality sculptures were done by fine artists. Many poor pieces were profusely marked. Some of the finest works contain no identifying marks whatsoever. The expert, therefore is not dependent on marks; to him they are but one criteria in evaluation. Only the novice is sold by what is written on the base of a statue.

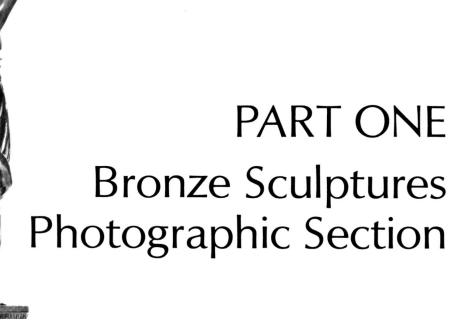

# PART ONE
## Bronze Sculptures
## Photographic Section

# Bronze Sculptures
## PHOTOGRAPHIC SECTION

*KEY TO NUMBERING SYSTEM: Photos are counted consecutively, from 100 through 799, with each figure assigned just one number.*

*CAPTION PAGES, interspersed among the photograph pages, contain capsulized information about each piece. They also contain miscellaneous information relative to the work, such as exhibitions, prizes won, unique characteristics, notes on founder or sculptor, etc.*

*BASIC DATA is presented in the following sequence: • Number of piece • Title • Sculptor • Date sculpted, actual or estimated ("Circa" abbreviated "c") • Country where cast (abbreviated: Fr.=France; Gr.=Germany; Aus.=Austria) • Color of finish ("Patina" abbreviated "Pt.") • Height of figure, in inches.*

*Whenever appropriate, resource or background information is presented preceding a specific or particular category of sculptures.*

100.  JESTER by Lafon Mollo
        c1900  Fr.  Pt: Dark Brown.  11"

The Jester is a lady! Specializing in royal
entertainment, she dances, sings and tells stories.
Sculpted in provocative, twirling pose, one can
almost hear the jingling of the bells on her skirt,
vest, cap and shoes. The stick with clown's head
(zany or bauble) is raised for all to see, while
her fan and tambourine remain secondary accessories. Coyly tilted head and dimpled smile
add to appeal of this charming, well-proportioned
subject.

**100**

105

109

113

116

105. PHRYNE
by Adolf-Karl-Johannes Brutt
1888. Ger. Pt: Red-brown. 22"

"Phryne" is cast in one piece and is solid through-out. Smooth finish; perfect in every detail, even down to her tiny fingernails. She stands semi-nude with a nonchalant expression, as if daring you to turn away. Was exhibited in 1893 at the World's Columbian Exposition in Chicago, in the North Court of the Central Pavilion in the Art Gallery Building.

109. AMAZON QUEEN by Rene Leger
1911. Fr. Pt: Gold brown. 17½"

"Amazon Queen", prize winner in Paris Salon, 1911, is hollow cast, with arms and legs perfectly fitted and pinned to torso. Strong-featured and muscular, yet beautiful and feminine. To truly appreciate its artistic beauty and craftsmanship, this work should be viewed from all sides. The "Amazon Queen" (Hippolyta) was the fiercest of the mythological female warriors; although described as single-breasted in story, in sculpture and art she's always rendered with her womanly attributes intact. In her hair she wears the moon of Diane the Huntress (Artemis), her patron god-dess.

113. VIGIL by Mathurin Moreau
c1905. Fr. Pt: Grn.-yellow. 18"

Uniquely constructed; figure of the mother is cast in four sections–fitted together at waist (dark circular fold) and where arms enter garment. "Vigil" is a graceful grouping in a pleasing, well-balanced composition. Set on a site overlooking the sea, it seems to convey a complete story. The mother (wife) watches the horizon for sign of a ship; the wind lashes her hair and face, and one can detect her worry and concern. The daughter instinctively clings to her mother, while the son, too young to sense the anxiety of the situation, angrily tries to free his arm from his mother's pro-tective grasp.

116. SISTERS
by Hippolyte-Francois Moreau
c1905. Fr. Pt: Choc. brn. 29"

Heavy statue; originally had marble base and swivel apparatus. "Sisters" captures mood of two young girls as they pause from filling basket latched to elder's back. As they gaze at the wonders of the sea, waves lick at their bare feet. The younger sister notices something in water; her eyes are wide and her mouth is open in excitement.

118. GARTER GIRL
c1910. Aus. Pt: Multi-color paint. 6"

Early pin-up girl subject. Lovely, full figure, wearing corset, ribbed stockings, period-styled pumps.

121. PIGGYBACK by Nam Greb.
c1910. Aus. Pt: Green and gold paint.

Joyous young bacchante riding off into the sunset on the shoulders of a single-minded young satyr. His hands, her toes, and both their expressions are superbly detailed.

122- Seven individual seals.
128. 1880-1920. Fr. & Ger. 2-3"
Seals pictured here are bronze, unsigned.

Seals are seldom signed; occasionally they will bear the initials or stamp of the maker. Seals were often given as gifts, with bottom left blank so that recip-ient could have it inscribed with his initials, coat of arms, or his official identifying mark.

130. BOUQUET
c1910. Aus. Pt: Multi-color paint. 4"

Young lad attired in Empire Period costume: double-breasted square-tailed coat, ruffled cuffs, breeches and top hat. Happy, confident smile; looks as if he might be calling at the front door of some young lady.

131. HELPER. Unsigned.
c1900. Fr. Pt: Brn. & gold. 4"

Realistic, shy, dirty-faced, nervous expression aptly captures the personality of this little workshop helper of the child labor days. This piece was used as a match holder.

133. CIGAR. Unsigned.
c1900. Ger. Pt: Gold paint. 4"

Facial expression is quite appropriate for this mis-chievous ragamuffin of the streets, who's quick at picking up bad habits.

Fig. 105.

118

121

122　　123　　124　　125　　126　　127　　128

130　　131　　133

136

138

140

142

148

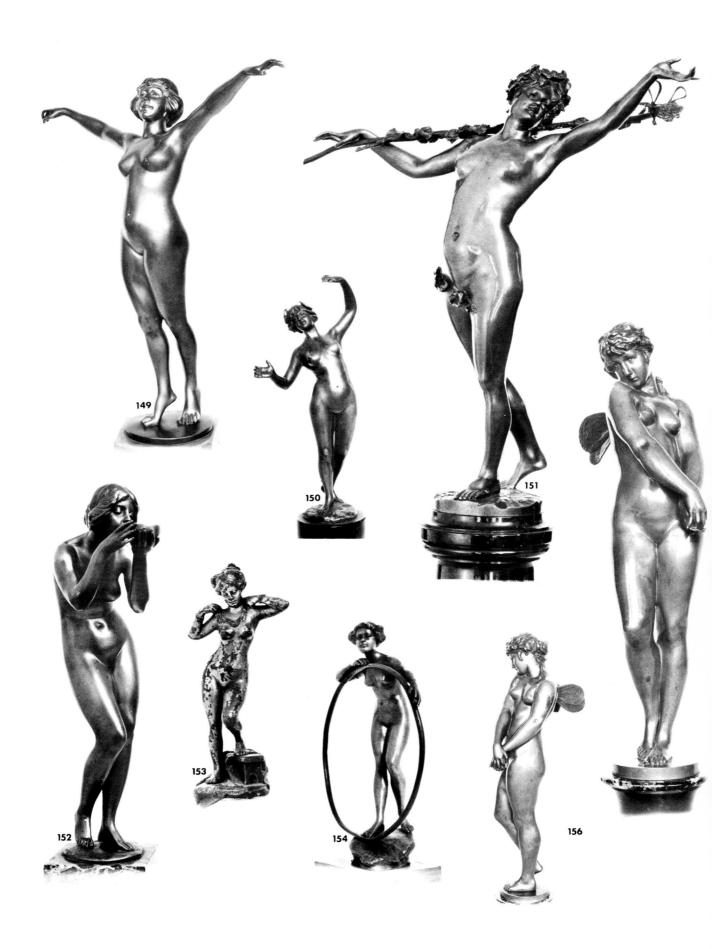

136. ANKLE BRACELETS by S. Wernekinck
c1925. Ger. Pt: 2-tone gold paint. 28"

This piece symbolizes the physical fitness fad prevailing in Germany during the 1920's. The lady, rendered in Art Deco style, appears to be practicing for her exercise class. Executed in fine, turn-of-the-century Gladenbeck and Sohn tradition, this is one of the last large bronzes hollow-cast with fitted arms and legs.

138. DECO DANCER by T. D. Guirande
c1925. Fr. Pt: Grn. & gold. 20"

Same period as that of Fig. 136, but with the French flavor; body clothed, legs closer together. S-shaped wreath contrasts markedly with 90-degree angles of left elbow and knee-sweep of gown. Toe and bottom flowers touch the base-- all the support that is needed for this perfectly balanced piece. Note Deco-style marble base in smaller photo at left. Extra fine detail is evident in hair, flowers, gown and right hand.

140. MIRROR, MIRROR by Pierre Roche
c1900. Fr. Pt: Dark green. 13"

Lovely Parisienne lady rendered in a rather subdued style, compared to Roche's more fanciful Art Nouveau figures of Loie Fuller. Interesting hairdo and draping of garment; good face and fingers. Note feet are not visible due to Art Nouveau draping of gown spilling onto base.

142. COMB by E. Saalmann
c1928. Ger. Pt: Green. 12"

Done in Art Deco style: stiff positioning of arms, lovely face, delicate hands, and slender figure. Modified octagon marble base (not shown) repeats shape of bronze base. High-gloss surface is achieved by fine chiseling and heavily lacquered patina.

148. SPRING by Peter Breuer
1890. Ger. Pt: Grn.-brn. 13"

Edited by Gladenbeck & Sohn foundry; their finest quality. Graceful, relaxed and lovely from every angle. Note treatment of eyes and hair and perfect form of left hand and both feet, especially toes (Supha).

*Peter Breuer
1890*

149. TIP TOES by B. Grundmann
c1923. Ger. Pt: Gold paint. 11"

Bold, proud stance; straight arms in Deco-period style. Finely chiseled surface; graceful; perfect fingers. Typical of the works being produced in Germany during its physical culture consciousness of the 1920's and 1930's.

150. SO BIG! by V. Seifert
c1910. Ger. Pt: Brown. 6"

Nude, beautifully executed; proud, healthy, and uninhibited. Position of fingers indicate that at one time the piece may have included an item in one or both hands.

151. BACCHANTE
by Bruno Friedrich Emile Kruse
c1895. Ger. Pt: Deep green. 11"

Exceptional quality is evidenced by satin finish, fine thin fingers and life-like palms. Mild, thoughtless expression befits role of the Bacchante in mythology.

152. THIRSTY by Victor Heinrich Seifert
c1900. Ger. Pt: Dark green. 11½"

Although somewhat coy, in the French style, this work is from the Gladenbeck foundry. One of Seifert's more gentle pieces; he is better known for his military subjects.

153. GOOD NIGHT by Bergman
c1905. Aus. Pt: Multi-color paint; gold body. 3½"

Tiny figure, removing her necklace, is gracefully posed. Perfect proportions; fully detailed face.

154. HOOP GIRL by Ruff
c1915. Ger. Pt: Green. 7"

Calm, relaxed expression; arms and legs chiseled to satin-smooth finish. Somewhat different from the typical nude.

156. PSYCHE by Paul Dubois
c1860. Fr. Pt: Bronze. 13"

Smooth finish. Face, hair and hands are exceptionally life-like. Body is rendered in the ideal female proportions of the time.

162

164

166

## HARLEQUIN

*Harlequin was a 16th century "Commedia Dell Arte" character, readily recognized by his mask and the diamond-shaped patches on his tights. He is generally depicted as lithe, athletic, witty, shrewd and amoral. Dancing, singing, comedy and drama were all part of his stagecraft and improvised performances. The slap-stick he carried was a prop for his feats of magic and for signaling scene changes. The character Columbine was the woman he loved; but, in matters of the heart he was regarded as a simpleton.*

162.  HARLEQUIN by Rene de Saint-Marceaux
      1879. Fr. Pt: Med. brown. 26"

In keeping with his role, harlequin stands looking down on the honest world, while a crooked, confident grin is evident on his handsome face. The eyes of this figure are crafted in rather a unique manner; hollow sockets behind the mask contain small, hanging appendages, which give the illusion of eyes peering at the viewer from all angles. Base of "Harlequin" simulates floor of a theatre. Original edition was cast by the Barbedienne Foundry in Paris and carries its seal of special quality, "Reduction Mecanique, A. Collas." "Harlequin" was produced both in smaller and larger editions, and under the same seal.

164.  LADY HARLEQUIN by Mestais
      c1890. Fr. Pt: Choc. brown. 18"

Lady harlequin in suggestive posture poses lifting mask and displays costume with low-cut blouse.

166.  HARLEQUIN by Paul Dubois
      c1880. Fr. Pt: Dark brown. 23"

Attired in typical harlequin costume, figure stands center stage and appears ready to do some magic or mischief with his slap-stick. Position of arms makes for pleasing composition.

# P.DVBOIS

168.  HOOKED! by Antoine Bofill
      1902. Fr. Pt: Grn-brn. 10"

This delightful piece was awarded second prize in the Paris Salon of 1902. Exhibited nude, it was modified for public consumption by founder Titre. Young fisherman happily examining his catch; interesting base shows water swooping over rocks.

170.  IMPROVISATEUR by Auguste Moreau
      1900. Fr. Pt: Dark brown. 13"

This charming, cupid-like figure won the Medal of Gold at the Paris Exposition of 1900. Portrayed with love-note clutched in hand and mandolin strapped to back; music scroll spills from base.

171.  LE DIABOLO by Goldscheider
      c1905. Fr. Pt: Gold. 11"

Leg and arm positioning lend action to figure of young boy, with long locks and curls, engrossed in a popular game of skill of the day.

172.  ZUT! by A. Colle
      c1890. Fr. Pt: Dark brown. 12½"

Sassy cupid, with typical little wings and bow, is thumbing nose, as if daring some adversary. Light and playful mood; sculpted as a frivolous fun piece.

174.  ALERTE by Auguste Moreau
      c1885. Fr. Pt: Choc. brown. 12"

Beware--cupid may be anywhere. Here he is, fully equipped and fully prepared, with bow, quiver, wings, and love-shield on arm. Posed on a double base, with title plaque.

168

170

171

172

174

175

176

178

180

181

182

### 175. BOY, BALL & LETTER
c1900. Aus. Pt: Natural bronze. 3½"

Very well done piece, considering size of figure.
Good features and facial expression. Hand and
ball are executed as a single element, eliminating
need for finger detailing.

### 176. TOOTHACHE by Sutton
c1880. Ger. Pt: Black. 7½"

Solid casting, cleverly executed. Unhappy subject,
realistically depicted, with pained expression and
swollen cheek.

### 178. STUDENT by Marcel Debut
c1895. Fr. Pt: Light bronze. 16"

Fine work, by the younger Debut, is cast hollow
in two main pieces connecting at the waist.
Simplicity of design draws attention to face.
Upper portion of base shows a sloping stone
walkway.

### 180. WINE by Vital-Cornu
c1885. Fr. Pt: Med. brown. 14"

Solid cast throughout, with arms connected at
shoulders. Young wine seller, captured in a color-
ful, candid pose. Sculpted with meticulous attention to texture and detail.

### 181- CROQUET by Franz Iffland
### 182. c1900. Ger. Pt: Lacq. bronze. 9"

Charming pair involved in a game of croquet. The
lady is daintily holding her gown clear of mallet,
as both figures concentrate intently on her shot.

## BARBEDIENNE

*M. FERDINAND BARBEDIENNE, the eminent
founder of the great Parisian house, has died in
his eighty-second year. Employed at a paper-
merchant's from 1832 to 1834, he was fortunate
enough in that year to make the acquaintance of a
clever artisan, ACHILLE COLLAS by name. The
latter had invented an instrument by which he
could accurately reproduce in full or reduced size
objects in the round or in relief. Barbedienne
quickly appreciated the value of the invention, and
combined forces with Collas for the working of his
patent. This resulted in the foundation of the
celebrated house of Barbedienne, which, giving
employment to six hundred workmen, has reproduced the great works of classic art in many of the
principal museums, as well as "published" the
works of the principal living sculptors of France.*

From obituary: Magazine of Art, 1892.

### 183. CANDELABRE by Ferdinand Barbedienne
1867. Fr. Pt: Dark brown. 32"

"Candelabre" is of Barbedienne's own design and
was exhibited by him in L'Exposition Universelle
1867. Its trim elegance begins with a triple gar-
goyle base, topped by a deity bust, a sectional
centre-post which branches into five candle-pots,
and a perching stork at the very peak. "Candelabre" disassembles into 32 pieces.

### 184- CANDLESTICK BASE
### 185. by Ferdinand Barbedienne
c1850. Fr. Pt: Gold dore & choc. br. 18"

Teasing, fearless babies, just inches away from
snapping reptiles, add interest to ornate bases,
which are identical except for babies. Bases are
cast in many sections and are fitted to accommodate various candle-pot arrangements.

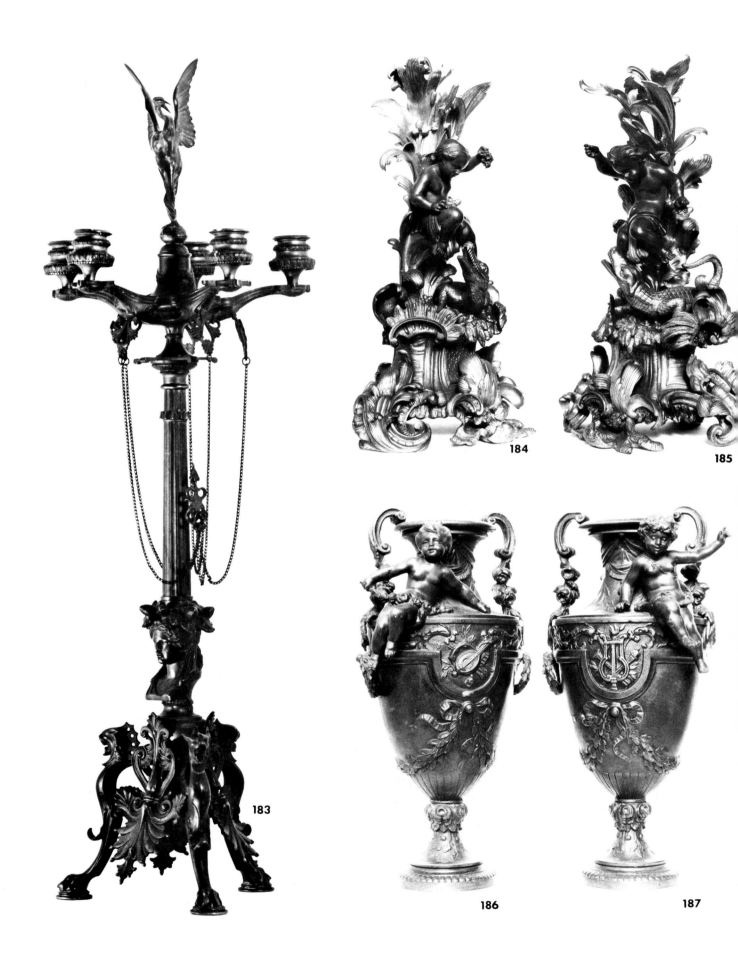

183

184

185

186

187

188

190

192

193

197

200

201

202

203

204     205

206

Fig. 200.

186- URNS (MUSICAL)
187. by Siot-Decauville Fondeurs
c1870. Fr. Pt: Green and brown.

These fine metal urns have the ring of glass and the weight of bronze. Plaques are musical, with alternate design on reverse side. Wreaths serve as handles. Babies are cast of a softer metal.

188. JARDINIERE. Attributed to Joseph Cheret
c1895. Fr. Pt: Natural gold color.
Planter, 12"; Boys, 7"

The four identical sides of planter are flawlessly brazed together at corners. Boys gracing corners are perfectly finished. Detail on planter is deep and hand-chiseled. Eight perfect hands and forty hand-chiseled fingernails (Supha) are visible when piece is turned over.

190. PLANTER by Maximilien-Victor Ringel
c1880. Fr. Pt: Gold dore. 6¼" x 16"

Elegant planter, with fruit-knob handles, shows parents and baby birds in nest on one side and baby's first flight on other side.

192. WATER-BABIES by Gustave-Joseph Cheret
1882. Fr. Pt: Gold bronze. 15"

Thirteen water-babies, in various degrees of relief, dangle precariously from gnarled branches which form handles. Babies, exhibiting expressions ranging from exuberance to fear, are pursued by gigantic frogs. This delightful piece was displayed as a lamp base in the Electrical Section of the 1882 Paris Exhibition.

193. URN. Unsigned.
Origin unknown. Pt: Grey to black. 18"

A most unique piece cast in nine sections of alternating iron and bronze. Every inch is filled with highly detailed scenes from 16th century slave trade and mythology. A relaxed satyr, with two ominous tentacles entwining his arms, form eerie handle.

197. GIVING. Unsigned.
c1780. It. or Fr. Pt: Trans. brown. 48"

Size and subject suggest this was a commissioned piece, perhaps for some large entranceway; at one time may have had a signed and dated male counterpart. Base, face, and chiseling technique combine to make it a unique work.

200. MASQUERADE
by Andre-Louis-Adolphe Laoust
1887. Fr. Pt: Choc. brown. 34"

At the moment of truth, masquerader's stance is bold and arrogant, his face radiant. Note oversized mask lying on ornamental base, which is key to this masquerade.

201. TRANQUILITY
by Vincent-Desire Faure de Brousse
c1870. Fr. Pt: Dark brown. 9"

Excellent example of Faure de Brousse's skill is this expressive study of a seated mother surrounded by her three admiring children.

202. LISSY ELKART by Carl Reiter
c1920. Ger. Pt: Brown. 4"

Introducing Miss Lissy Elkart; cast in Munich.

203. A KISS by Auguste Moreau
c1900. Fr. Pt: Brn. & grn. paint. 8"

Delicate, decorative subject with both arms free and one foot extending off base. Though cast in white metal, this piece could easily pass as bronze.

204- TEARS AND JEERS by Louis Kley
205    c1875. Fr. Pt: Silver-black. 5"

Boys, in miniature, set on matched red marble bases. "Tears" has ripped seat of his pants, while "Jeers" thinks it very amusing. From studio of L. Kley, a name often seen on cleverly contrived bronzes.

206. MOTHER by Jean-Jacques Pradier
c1825. Fr. Pt: Brown. 9"

Variation of the popular mother-child groups. Three figures are alert, with attention focused on one another rather than in several directions. Twist of body of standing child shows influence of classical style.

**210**

213

214

216

217

# A·CARRIER

**210. ENTRE DEUX AMOURS**
by Albert Ernest Carrier Belleuse
c1878. Fr. Pt: Dark green. 28"

A controversial piece in its day, by one of the period's most imaginative sculptors. Originally done in marble, this attractive and voluptuous young mother is indeed "between two loves" -- romantic and maternal love.

# H. LeVasseur

**213. SLEEPING** by Henri-Louis Le Vasseur
c1880. Fr. Pt: Dark brown. 24"

Madonna-like young mother typifies maternal protectiveness and gentleness. Quietly, yet powerfully, Le Vasseur captures the essence of a mother's infinite love and patience.

# E. Picault

**214. DRUMMER** by Emile-Louis Picault
c1885. Fr. Pt: Brown. 25"

Youthful, 15th century drummer-piper has strong features, high cheek-bones, characteristic of the many male figures sculpted by Picault during his lengthy career.

**215. RATMAN** by E. Bartlet
c1860. Aus. Pt: Silver black. 8"

This small figure, in Gothic attire and employed in an unenviable occupation, has four "victims" hooked to his pouch. At his foot is a fifth rodent, which he is enticing with his tunes. Garment texture and facial features are superbly detailed.

**217. PIED PIPER OF HAMLIN**
c1910. Aus. Pt: Multi-color enamel. 8"

The piper plays his way around the edge of black marble ash-tray, closely followed by three small music-lovers.

218

219

220

221

222

223

224

225

227

228

229

218. FOOTED BOWL on marble base. Two handles and lid formed by birds in nest. By Barbedienne Foundry. c1880. Fr. Pt: Brown. 7"

219. FIGURE holding two glass candy bowls; Art Nouveau. c1925. Amer. Pt: Green enamel. 9"

220. INKSTAND with wood inset under design on lid; Art Nouveau. c1910. Amer. Pt: Yellow. 3"

221. BACCHANTE, miniature, with pine cone and grapes; Art Nouveau. c1910. Aus. Pt: Green. 3½"

222. CLOWN INKWELL with head through hoop and mouth that opens. c1920. Amer. Pt: Yellow. 2"

223. INK STAND with tray and head of Dutch girl. c1910. Ger. Pt: Black. 3"

224. BOOKEND, white metal, of maiden drinking at spring. By L. & F. Moreau. c1905. Fr. Pt: Grey. 8"

225. INKWELL, etched Art Nouveau design. Incised signature of Marshall Field & Company, Chicago. c1910. Amer. Pt: Yellow. 4"

227. ARABIAN DANCER with moveable skirt, on marble ash-tray. By Bergman. c1910. Aus. Pt: Multi-colored enamel. 5"

228. DISH, with shape formed by lady's dress; Art Nouveau. By Rubin. c1915. Amer. Pt: Gold. 3"

229. DESK SET, 5-piece: stamp box, ink-well, paper clamp, letter opener and tray. c1915. Amer. Pt: Lt. brown. 3"

231. MATCH BOX HOLDER and ash-tray with lady; Art Nouveau/Art Deco. c1920. Amer. Pt: Green. 4½"

232. ASH-TRAY with young girl in long coat and muff. By Hafner. c1910. Aus. Pt: Black. 5"

233. WATER GIRL with yoke. (Buckets missing). c1910. Aus. Pt: Brown. 3"

234. BOWL with pedestal and leaf-motif handles. By Siot (Founder). c1900. Fr. Pt: Brown. 5"

235. PETITE ARTIST sitting on pallet with brushes atop paint-box. By August-Edme Suchetet. c1895. Fr. Pt: Grn., gold & blk. 4"

236. INFANT perched on round base. By More. 1905. Ger. Pt: Green. 4"

237. VASE with face and floral design. By Jacques Callot. Prize-winner, 1898. Fr. Pt: Grn. 8½"

238. MATCH BOX HOLDER and ash-tray; Art Nouveau. By C. J. Hiller. c1900. Amer. Pt: Green. 6"

239. CARD DISH on pedestal; base adorned with 3 Bacchus Babies; mythological panorama on inner surface of dish. c1825. Fr. Pt: Black-green. 12"

240. PEACE by J. Kassin 1908. Fr. Pt: Gold bronze. 18"

A symbolic work, with woman's arm clutching sword covered by palm branch, while her other hand holds a small lantern. Smaller recasts of "Peace", with little detail, were produced during World War I.

241. LE PREMIER PRIX by C. Anfrie 1888. Fr. Pt: Brown. 17"

Young lady in contemporary attire and long leather gloves waves hat. Her attention appears to be focused on someone far in front of statue.

240

241

LE PREMIER PRIX

242

244

246

248

249

251

262

263

264

265

242. BEATRICE by Lucien Pallez
c1885. Fr. Pt: Black. 13"

Wearing floral patterned dress, which gracefully falls to a base inscribed with her name, lovely Beatrice stands with rose cupped in hand.

244. SPHINX by T. Herlinger
1904. Fr. Pt: Grn (Sphinx) & brn (nude). 6" x 8"

Erotic work of nude with flowing hair provocatively perched on Sphinx. This top quality bronze was given away as a sales promotion item.

246. KISSING. Unsigned.
c1825. Fr. Pt: Yellow-brn. 6"

A rarely portrayed female satyr is depicted seducing an unprotesting bacchante.

248. LE TREFLE by Antoni
c1895. Fr. Pt: Grey. 17"

"The Clover," an Art Nouveau white-metal piece, rivals the finest bronze of its type. Figure stands on a marble base with bronze plaque and has jointed arms and deep hand-chiseled features.

249. ON STAGE by Paul Tillet
c1890. Fr. Pt: Brn. enamel. 16½"

White-metal figure, cast in five sections--arms and legs fitted to torso. Graceful young lady has plucked a rose from her dress and offers it to you. Roses, leaves, fingers and petticoats (underside) are perfectly detailed.

251. PETITE MIMI by Nicolas Lecornet
c1885. Fr. Pt: Grey-brown. 25"

Surface of this most life-like bronze has the feel of satin. Young girl with flower basket on arm and holding a bouquet in each hand has a pleading expression, as if asking you to buy her flowers.

252. ON THE FENCE.
c1900. Fr. Pt: Choc. brown. 4"

Miniature desk piece with fully developed features on fingernail-size faces.

253. TWIRLING.
c1870. Fr. Pt: Natural tarnish. 5"

Around and around we go. Fine balance and much handwork on this happy little piece.

254. SPINNING.
c1910. Ger. Pt: Black. 8"

Parlor table piece of happy Dutch girls at play.

255. DECORATING by Jean Jacques Pradier
c1850. Fr. Pt: Brownish yellow. 13"

Great attention to detail is evident by hair texture and folds of woman's gown.

256. READING by Emile-Francois Fouquet
c1850. Fr. Pt: Black. 14"

Hair, face, hands and feet of lady intently reading are beautifully finished.

257. JACQUELINE by Mathurin Moreau
c1875. Fr. Pt: Yellow bronze. 21"

Realistic hairdo has deeply etched curls. Thin cast makes piece surprisingly light in weight for its size. This sitting figure is one of M. Moreau's fine early works.

262. FLOWER FAIRIES by Mathurin Moreau
c1875. Fr. Pt: Brown & gold. 39"

Beautifully modeled female and cherub-type flying figures, done in the classical style, are dreamily "flowering the earth." Simulated skin-texture achieved by careful knurling of the bronze surface.

263. YARN AND SPOOL
c1880. Fr. Pt: Gold bronze. 2½"

Solid cast. Well proportioned and finely detailed, considering its small size.

264. SITTING
c1880. Fr. Pt: Dark brown. 7"

Excellent hair and face. Arms attached under bracelets.

265. DREAMING
By Alexandre-Pierre Schoenewerk
c1850. Pt: Brown. 6" x 12"

Draped garment conveys feeling of transparency. Hands, hair, necklace, and expression are all excellent.

Fig. 251.

269

274

269.  L'EMIR by Marie-Alexandre-Lucien Coudray
      c1890.  Fr.  Pt: Dark brown.  31"

"L'Emir" is a powerfully built, nomadic, middle-
eastern chieftain, suggestive of type that fought
against crusaders.  His piercing eyes, beard and
broad shoulders, leather vest and robe, long curv-
ing sword, and pointed footwear all compel one's
attention.  Ornate bronze base contains seal and
inscribed plaque from Exposition des Beau Arts.

274.  TAHOSER
      by Marie-Alexandre-Lucien Coudray
      1893.  Fr.  Pt: Chocolate.  26"

Lovely Egyptian entertainer, powerfully built in
the Coudray style, wears Royal Egyptian headdress (Uraeus) with asp.  Twelve-string harp base
features head of sphinx, a beautiful bronze in itself.
Base also contains bronze guarantee seal and a
plaque.  "Tahoser" won the coveted prize of Rome
in 1893.

277.  A LA MER by Beyard de la Vingtrie
      c1905.  Fr.  Pt: Sea-green.  34"

Pretty subject, clad in bathing-attire of the period,
is captured gingerly lowering herself from a rock
to the water.  Presented by sculptor in a most
unique way -- arms and legs are free and outstretched, while woman's back is bent and all four
limbs are behind her.

279.  "DUMP HER IN"
      c1905.  Aus.  Pt: Multi-color enamel.  7½"

Man lifts his lady, runs to edge of pier, and is about
to toss her into the lake.  She reacts, of course, in
typical feminine fashion, by kicking, yelling and
laughing.  Very expressive piece is perfect for its
small size.  Heavy, circular marble-base ash-tray,
with light and dark brown swirls in grain, gives an
illusion of water.

277

279

282

286

282. LE DECOUVERTE by Lenberti Sua
    c1902. Fr. Pt: Choc. brn; gold trim. 24"

"The Discovery" captures mood of the occasion. Pretty young girls are attired in newest swimwear fashion of the day.

286. PREMIER BAIN DE MER by G. Wagner
    c1900. Fr. Pt: Dk. brn. over deep red. 34"

"Baby's First Bath in the Sea" is a delightful experience. Most striking is contrast in expression between mother and child; mother's motion or intent doesn't seem to be hampered by struggling infant. Base is ornamented with various creatures of the sea.

289. THE NET by Waagen
    c1905. Fr. Pt: Grey paint. 29"

Handsome fisherman in straw hat readies net as young assistant steadies boat. Although produced as promotion giveaway to participating taverns by beer company, piece is of quality craftsmanship.

290- DUTCH CHILDREN BOOK-ENDS
291. c1900. Aus. Pt: Brown. 4"

Fine detail and facial expression in solid cast miniature Dutch figures, only 2" tall. Base of book-ends are hollow and lead-filled.

292- CAVALIERS by Thom.-Anatole Guillot
293. c1895. Fr. Pt: Grey. 8"

Cavalier at left, with hand on sword, proposes a toast. Cavalier at right strikes a nonchalant pose as he strokes moustache. Fine detail for figures of this size.

294- CONQUISTADORES
295. c1910. Fr. Pt: Green paint. 10"

Mint condition of pair of white metal figures is evident in photo. Fabrication Francais seal and wood bases offer only clues in identifying metal used.

**289**

**290**      **291**

**292**      **293**

**294**      **295**

299

300

303

301

## VILLANIS

*Emmanuele Villanis (or Villani) was perhaps the most prolific sculptor of the late Victorian/early Art Nouveau period. Although born in Italy, he did most of his work in France, where his sculptures were generally cast under the seal of the Society of Bronzes in Paris.*

*In the late 1880's, after his initial successes, Villanis shunned the exhibit and salon circuits. It was said that he became an industry unto himself, and that his hundreds of bronzes are what helped keep France solvent in the 1880's and 1890's.*

*Villanis' works are almost exclusively of female subjects. His bust sculptures, which outnumber his production of full figures by perhaps 20 to one, are easily recognized by the artistic scrolling of the subject's name below her face. Also readily identifiable as Villanis are the perfect, ideally proportioned features of his women's faces; and adjectives such as "serious, reflective, serene, detached, madonna-like" are among those that best describe their facial expressions. To achieve a more realistic quality in the faces he sculpted, Villanis used a deep cut for the eyes——a technique in sharp contrast to other sculptors of the time who tried to reproduce the natural eyeball.*

*Although his works are everywhere, little is known about the man behind the goddess-like heads. Probably 300-500 of Villanis' bronzes are presently in existence——a quantity challenged only by Van Der Straeten and the combined works of the Moreaus. Many of Villanis' pieces done in metal and chalk can still be found in shops today.*

**299. PAPILLON** by Emmanuele Villanis c1890. Fr. Pt: Translucent lt brn. 31½"

"Papillon" won Medaille D'or in Paris in 1890. It is certainly Villanis' artistic skill at its best: wings, rose-base, hands, body, face all beautifully executed. Papillon (meaning "butterfly" in French) represents Psyche, the beautiful maiden loved by and later married to Cupid .

**300. AURORA** by Emmanuele Villanis. c1895. Fr. Pt: Brown paint. 15"

Although this particular cast is unsigned, the proud face unmistakenly identifies it as a work of Villanis. "Aurora," goddess of dawn, flimsily clad in New Art draping of ancient Greek garment, is well-formed and somewhat more robust than Psyche.

**301. DALILA** by Emmanuele Villanis. c1890. Fr. Pt: Shades of brown. 16"

"Dalila," cast under seal of Society of Bronzes, is numbered and initialed by foundryman. Attractive multi-color patina shows face to great advantage. Deep-set eye cavities make "Dalila" interesting to view in changing light and from different angles. Extremely life-like.

**303. ARTIST** by Emmanuele Villanis. c1895. Fr. Pt: Med. brown. 29"

Statue rests on a unique, swivel-style base. New Art is evident in draping of garment. Observe similarity of leg-positioning to that of "Papillon".

### WHITE—METAL BUSTS

*French, medium-sized, fine quality, turn-of-the-century, white-metal painted busts. All in grouping are of sufficient thickness to weigh and to "ring" the same as bronzes of comparable size. Each piece was hand-filed to eliminate mold flashing. When original patina of white metal busts in this category are in good condition, upon superficial examination they are indistinguishable from bronzes.*

304. CELIA. Unsigned. 11½"
305. SAPHO by Villanis. 12" & 16"
306. SOPHIA by A. de Ranieri. 14"
307. VICTORIA by Ernest Ferrard. 10½"
308. ZORA by E. Villanis. 9½" & 12"
309. AMY by Ralph Lillo. 17"
310. LYS by Theophile Somme. 16"
311. KAREN by Dutrion. 13"

304    305    306    307    308

309    310

311

318

**320**

**321**

**319**

**322**

**323**

**326**

314. AMAZON by Karl-August-Eduard Kiss
     c1860. Ger. Pt: Brown. 16"

In this group terrified horse is attacked by tiger. Amazon takes careful aim to dispatch tiger with one thrust. First exhibited in 1839 in Berlin, where it gained extensive popularity among the citizenry. Collections were taken up to produce a life-sized bronze replica; in 1845, one was erected at entrance to the Royal Museum.

In 1851 a giant, copper-plated zinc casting of "Amazon," by the Geiss Foundry of Berlin, won a prize at the London Exposition. Afterwards, it was shipped to America and exhibited at the New York Crystal Palace, in 1853, where it was destroyed in a fire.

The solid-cast bronze shown here is an early, reduced version, by Gladenbeck and Sohn Foundry.

## RUSSIAN BRONZES

*Russian bronzes, with their fine detail and overall casting excellence, are a specialized field of collecting/investing. Most of the pieces on the market today were cast in St. Petersburg, between 1850-1900, and are well marked.*

*Although their superb quality has long been recognized, Russian bronzes were out of vogue during the years between the two World Wars. The very statues that went begging in 1943 at $100 are now snapped up at auction for $5,000. Prospective buyers, however, should be cautious of the magic in the word "Russian"; it is not synonymous with top quality. Russia, just as other countries, produced bronzes that varied in craftsmanship and quality. Only through careful examination, and experience, can one learn to judge and select the finest works.*

318. COSSACK PLUNDER
     by Ievgueni-Alexandrovitch Lanceray
     c1874. Rus. Pt: Black. 18"

The story depicted here is one of murder. The expressionless Cossack wipes blood from blade on his horse's mane as slain rider's horse, terror in his eyes, seems to call out for his dead master. Finest of detail on figure, animals, horses' gear, etc. "Cossack Plunder" exemplifies the best of Russian quality.

319. BASKET—PEEP by A. Titze
     c1900. Aus. Pt: Painted. 4"

Small ornamental bronze of excellent quality wired to ring bell in servants' quarters.

320. FLOWER PICKER by Franz-Adolph Sautner
     c-1900. Aus. Pt: Yellow bronze. 5"

Wire from ivory and bronze rose under base connects to servants' quarters.

## DIANE THE HUNTRESS

*Artemis, or Diane, twin sister of Apollo, is one of the original twelve major deities in Greek/Roman mythology. Her representations in art and sculpture are surpassed in quantity only by Cupid. Diane is goddess of light, healing, childbirth, etc., but she is most commonly depicted as a huntress, with bow and a dog at her side. Bodily she appears as a slim, supple young maiden, with hair partly gathered in back, and knotted, and with a moon ornament adorning it.*

321. DIANE by Emmanuele Villanis
     c1900. Fr. Pt: Grn.-brown. 4"
     Also produced in larger sizes: 8", 12", 16".

322. DIANE
     c1900. Fr. or Ger. Pt: Dark brown. 3"

323. DIANE by Georges Van-Der-Straeten
     c1900. Fr. Pt: Med. brown. 18"

Bow cradles red marble column. Also was cast in a smaller 12" version.

326. YOUTH AND LEOPARD by Loys Potet
     c1900. Fr. Pt: Brown & grn. paint. 18"

Stabbed leopard is shown giving his last snarl; blood is visible behind his left foreleg. Youth, confident but cautious, has just removed dagger. This piece won first Gold Medal at the Paris Exposition of 1900.

327

328

329

330

331

332

333

334

335

336

337

338

339

340

341

342

343

327. WHINNY by Pierre-Jules Mene
c1860. Fr. Pt: Dark yellow. 7"

Neighing horse is sculpted walking in meadow
alongside an old fence. Incised at his left foreleg,
in deep heavy lettering, is the name "P.J. Mene."

328. GREYHOUND by Pierre-Jules Mene
c1850. Fr. Pt: Dark brown. 5"

Head and base of this unsigned, old recast are fine,
but rear of hind legs show mold marks, paws lack
detail of the original, and chasing on ribs and back
are unfinished.

329. RABBITS
c1900. Ger. Pt: Light brown. 2½"

Mother, father and two baby rabbits are cast separately and welded together to form a whimsical
desk-piece.

330. PLOW HORSE
by Antoine-Louis Barye
c1840 Fr. Pt: Brown. 3"

Perfect miniature, also produced in an 8" version,
has in detail what it lacks in ferocity common to
most Barye pieces.

331. STAG
c1900. Aus. Pt: Brown & grn. paint. 4½"

Realistic rendering of stag standing at water's edge
which, for practical purposes, is for use as an ash-
tray; match-holder is at rear of figure.

332. BULL DOG
c1910. Aus. Pt: Dark brown. 1½"

One of many fine bronze miniature dogs cast in
the early 20th century for use as paperweights,
ash-trays, etc.

333. RIDING-HORSE
by Marie-Rosalie Bonheur
c1870. Fr. Pt: Grey. 5"

Simple study of standing horse exhibits excellent
veining on animal's legs and face.

334. STAG AND DOE
c1890. Fr. Pt: Brown paint. 7"

Excellent composition and fine study of two animals forming one piece. Cast in white metal, not
bronze, but workmanship and patina defy detec-
tion of this fact.

335. BUFFALO on inkstand with two hinged
wells and pen tray.
c1910. Aus. Pt: Black. 5" x 12"

336. BEAR molded around black marble ash-tray.
c1910. Aus. Pt: Yellow-brn. 3½"

337. DOGS on inkstand with hinged well and pen
tray.
c1910. Aus. Pt: Black. 3" x 9"

338. BIRD on planter with spider and web.
By A. F. Sautner.
c1910. Aus. Pt: Light brown. 6" x 10"

339. KING OF BEASTS snarling.
By Thomas-Francois Cartier.
Copyright: 1909. Fr. Pt: Grn. & brn.
11" x 23"

340. MOOSE. Des. by Jos. F. Rallenberg.
c1910. Aus. Pt: Brown. 5"

341. SPREAD EAGLE on granite.
c1910. Fr. Pt: Gold bronze. 9" (wing-span)

342. STAG on mountain.
By T. Curtz.
c1910. Aus. Pt: Gold & green enamel. 5"

343. PHEASANT against pines ash-tray
and match holder.
c1910. Ger. Pt: Yellow bronze. 4"

345. TOASTING HER SATYR
by Claude-Michel Clodion
c1850. Fr. Pt: Green-brown. 22"

Nicely interacting figures, with satyr balanced on
right hoof and bacchante on left foot. Customary
wine festival accessories appear on base--pine cone,
Syrinx (pan-pipes) and tambourine. Wine cup is
missing from bacchante's hand.

349. DOWN THE PATH. Unsigned.
c1800. Fr. Pt: Black. 20"

Very old and extremely fine casting. A subtle
erotic piece depicting a lecherous satyr leading a
naive bacchante down the wrong path. Cymbals
and vase decorate an otherwise plain base.

**345**

**349**

354

357

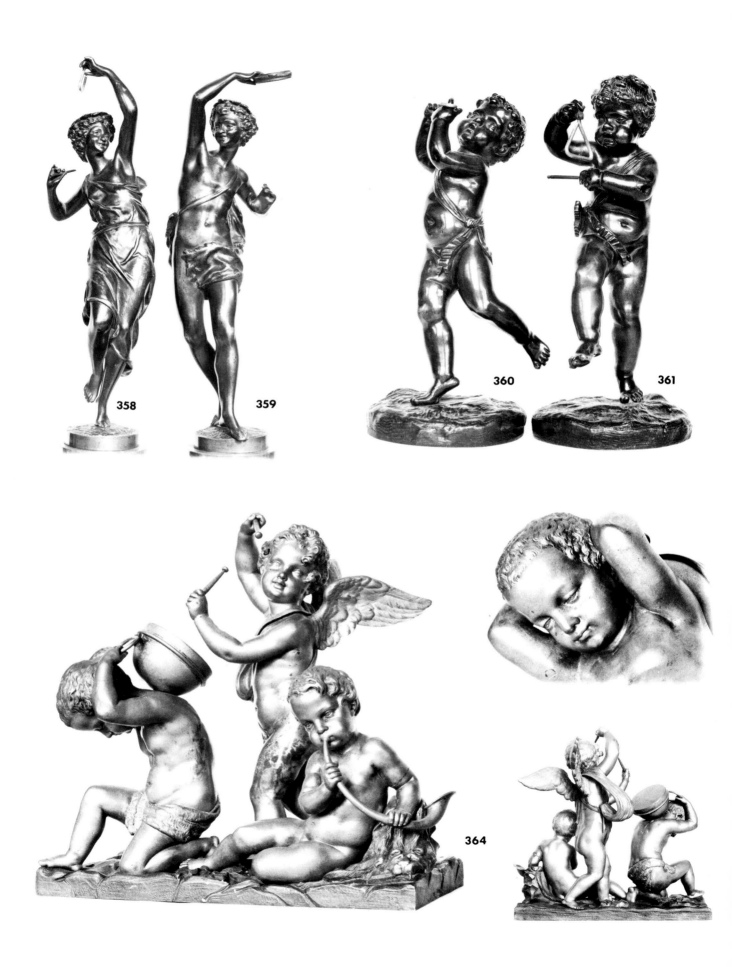

358    359    360    361

364

FAURE DE BROUSSE
PARIS
A B

#### 354. PANDORA AND MERCURY
by Faure de Brousse
c1875. Fr. Pt: Green. 27"

Mercury is flying high with Pandora, world's first woman created to punish man. The beautiful Pandora is gently holding box containing evils of the world--sorrow, sickness, pain, envy, jealousy, pride, hunger, poverty and want. According to mythological lore, Hepheastus, under orders by Zeus, molded Pandora from water and clay into a ravishing beauty, with human voice and life.

For grace, beauty, and technical brilliance, Faure de Brousse's sculpture is one of the finest of its type. Its two figures are balanced solely by Mercury's toes touching the base. This complex feat was attained by hollow-casting Mercury's foot and toes as part of base and joining them, as a unit, at his thigh; this gave the piece its needed strength.

#### THE GOD OF LOVE

*Called "Eros" in Greek and "Cupid" in Roman mythology, the god of love is the most common- ly portrayed deity. He is usually sculpted with bow, his mother Venus, his lover Psyche, or his young lady worshippers, the willing victims of his arrows.*

*Cupid's existence may be divided into three identifying periods: (1) as a baby--mischievous (506,512), repentent (508,509), and decorative (513); (2) as a young boy--teasing (172), danger- ous (174), proud (507), and lover's confidant (510); (3) as a man, with large beautiful wings, a supple athletic body, curly hair, and handsome face (517). When shown with his lover Psyche, Cupid is portrayed as attentive and protective (357).*

#### 357. CUPID AND PSYCHE
by Henri Godet
1898. Fr. Pt: Lt. brn. & gold. 31"

Godet's remarkable "Cupid and Psyche" was first exhibited at the Paris Salon des Beau Arts in 1898. Inspiration for this work came from painting by W. Bouguereau, which is acknowledged on base. Simulated rock formations at figures' feet are leaning back to counterbalance forward thrust of their bodies. Cupid's arms are protectively enfold- ing his love as they prepare to fly to his secret castle. Legend has it he would visit her nightly there, but Psyche's curiosity resulted in an abrupt end to that arrangement. (See Fig. 517).

Greek mythology also relates that Cupid's mother, Venus, who was jealous of Psyche, sent him to earth to pierce her heart with an arrow. This wound would then compel Psyche to fall hope- lessly in love with a monstrous creature, thus re- moving her permanently from the sight of men, who had come to believe she was the most beauti- ful of all women. But Cupid, god of love, at first sight of this radiant mortal, becomes so possessed and befogged by her beauty, he accidentally pierces himself with his own arrow.

Consistent with myth, Godet's Psyche is shy and beautiful and has butterfly wings sprouting from her back, her identifying characteristic in art and sculpture.

#### 358- HARMONIE by Ernest Rancoulet
359. c1875. Fr. Pt: Med. brown. 13"

Tall, graceful, happy figures; excellent faces. Tall, round, column-like marble base (not shown) adds 6" to height. This type of piece was used to adorn mantles and early-make pianos.

#### 360- MUSICIANS. Unsigned
361. c1825. Fr. Pt: Dark brown. 8½"

Lively little musicians dancing lightly on their toes. Used as ornaments for music room. Fine quality recasts of these figures made in last half of 19th century were signed Clodion.

#### 364. CUPID'S BAND. Unsigned.
c1830. Fr. Pt: Gold dore. 12"

Imaginative, decorative table piece. Three separ- ate figures are superbly finished. Cupid, center of attraction, pounds loudly for your attention. Not to detract from musical scene, figures are set on simple rectangular base.

366          368          370

371

372

373

374

376

**377**

**378**

**379**

**380**

**381**

**382**

**383**

**384**

## VAN DER STRAETEN

*Georges (or Joris) Van Der Straeten was born in 1857 in Ghent, Belgium. As a young man, he studied law during the day and sculpture at night. Love of the art, however, surpassed the desire to continue his career as an attorney. By 1878 he became one of Brussels' most prolific sculptors.*

*Van Der Straeten moved on to Paris, upon advice of his friend, Jan Van Beers, the renown painter. His renderings of small subjects, such as ragamuffins, pierrots, clowns, circus performers, etc., brought immediate success to him in this famed city. Van Der Straeten also gained recognition for his portrait busts of contemporary notables, as well as for sculptures of buxom peasant girls and seductive Parisian ladies. His skill in capturing facial expression was uncanny; under his talented touch, clay seemed to turn into flesh.*

*Most of Van Der Straeten's bronzes were cast under the seal of the Society of Bronzes, Paris. His signed pieces carried the initial "J" and his surname, scratched carelessly into the original clay.*

*Over his long career more than a thousand of Van Der Straeten's works were cast in bronze, with bust studies far outnumbering his full-length figures.*

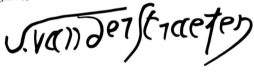

366- By Georges (or Joris) Van Der Straeten
376: 1880-1900. Fr. Pt: Shades of brown
Some editions were cast in larger and/or smaller sizes than shown.

366. JAN. – 13"

368. MAY – 16"

370. APRIL – 18"

371. JUNE – 8"

372. GEORGIE – 6"

373. JULIE – 7"

374. SONJA – 7"

376. SOUBRETTE – 16"

377. NAPOLEON I. Unsigned.
c1900. Fr. Pt: Yellow. 3"
Napoleon I, Emperor of France, posed in familiar uniform and in typical stance. Cabinet miniature.

378. JOAN OF ARC by Emmanuel Fremiet
c1870. Fr. Pt: Dk. brn. 7"
Joan of Arc, after her victory at Orleans. "Armed and placed at the head of 10,000 men, she inspired fervor where there was gloom."

379. JOAN OF ARC by Raoul Larche
c1890. Fr. Pt: Lt. brn. 10"
Joan is depicted here as a humble, deeply religious shepherdess in her early teens. One of several highly acclaimed "Joans" by Larche, popular sculptor of the New Art School.

380. LONGFELLOW. Unsigned.
c1910. Fr. Pt: Dk. grn. paint. 2"
Tiny bust of the famous American poet Henry Wadsworth Longfellow (1807-1882). Good quality; rendered in white metal on a black slate base.

381. MEYERBEER by Jean-Antoine Houdon
c1875. Fr. Pt: Trans. lt. brn. 2½"
Well-done, sub-miniature bronze faithfully duplicates expression and detail of original, larger than life-size work. Giacomo Meyerbeer (1791-1864) was a gifted German composer of songs, operas, choral music and instrumental works.

382. KING HENRY IV ENFANT
by baren Francois-Joseph Bosio
c1825. Fr. Pt: Brown. 18½"
Elegant statuette of the popular French monarch "Henry the Great" as a boy. Several editions and variations of this well-liked work were cast during the 19th century.

383. KING HENRY IV ENFANT
by baren Francois-Joseph Bosio
c1825. Fr. Pt: Lt. brn. & gold. 16"
Handsome bust of Henry IV, from full figure. Emblem is mounted on bronze base. Cast by Berneau, Paris.

384. SCHILLER. Unsigned.
c1900. Fr. Pt: Green. 5"
Souvenir, white-metal bust of Johann Schiller, German dramatist, poet, historian and philosopher.

387

388

**389**

**393**

# E. LoRMIER

### 387. UN INCROYABLE by Edouard Lormier
c1885. Fr. Pt: Brown. 26"

"Un Incroyable" was the name for young "fops" or "dandies" of the French Revolutionary period. These fashionable extremists wore double-breasted, square-tailed coats that hung below the knees. Often their huge white neckcloths were wrapped over their chins, as shown here. The twisted cane completed the total "in-look" of the times.

### 388- WHERE? THERE! by Carl Kauba
### 389. c1910. Ger. Pt: Rich copper. 8½"

Scottish couple sitting together on rocks tells a simple and complete story. Expressions and features on tiny faces are lifelike. Various textures on tam-o-shanters, vest, dress, and gloves are hand-chiseled. Kauba's versatility and attention to detail are evident throughout. Its original common base and plaque are not shown.

### 393. ADVENTURESS by Eutrope Bouret
c1900. Fr. Pt: Grn. & brn. 23½"

"Adventuress" glances from side to side as she carefully lifts her skirt and places a foot on first rock leading across stream. Flowers, used as an adornment in her hair, indicate New Art influence on Victorian sculptor Bouret.

# Pierre Ogé

### 396. SOUVENIR A GOUNOD
by Pierre-Marie-Francois O'ge
c1885. Fr. Pt: Green. 40"

O'ge's work is based on Gounod's opera "Faust." Marguerite, the lovely and simple maiden of the story, is sculpted picking petals from a daisy, while towering above her is a masterful bust of the French composer Gounod. Figure and bust have been cast separately in larger and smaller versions. This work, which combines the two, along with an added column, was a commissioned piece.

397 398 399 400

401

402

403

404

405

406

407

408

409

410

411

## BOYS (397-411)

*Children, particularly boys, because of their relative scarcity, are highly desirable items for bronze collectors. Presented here are 15 boy subjects in a variety of situations.*

**397. PROBESCHLUCK by K. Hackstock**
    c1900. Ger. Pt: Black. 9"

Small boy and big stein present an interesting contrast for "Testing the Brew."

**398. HEAVY BASKET by Louis-Ernest Barrias**
    c1880. Fr. Pt: Choc. 5½"

Herculean effort by baby as he raises basket and achieves this perfect balance. Original edition cast and signed by Barbedienne.

**399. BABY BACCHUS by Louis-Ernest Barrias**
    c1875. Fr. Pt: Yellow-brn. 9"

Welcome to the wine festival. Exquisite detail on fingers and hair. Arms are cast separately and attached at shoulders. Trace of lead reveals that object is missing from right hand.

**400. TEASING by Auguste Moreau**
    c1900. Fr. Pt: Painted. 9"

Delightful lamp base and ring tray. Boy appears more interested in proding lizard on side of fountain than in filling his jug. White-metal.

**401. SAILOR–BOY by J. Garnier**
    c1905. Ger. Pt: Dark brn. 16½"

Scotch sailor-boy dancing. Fine face and sleek finish. Positioning of arms simplifies casting. A rare piece from the Sanson Foundry in Hamburg.

**402. ACQUIS by Francois Roger**
    c1885. Fr. Pt: Dark brn. 16½"

Lad competes in game of skill, and judging from his facial expression, he has been quite successful at it.

**403. TOP SPINNER by Charles Lemarquier**
    c1900. Fr. Pt: Brn. enamel. 23"

Fine multiple casting, with arms and legs attached at elbow and knees. Note delicate fingers on this skilled spinner. Metal is not bronze, but is of excellent quality.

**404. CRYING**
    c1900. Aus. Pt: Yellow-brn. 2½"

This tiny fellow with kerchief and books under arm is sculpted in great detail, which is rather uncommon in pieces of this small size.

**405. SMOKING**
    c1900. Aus. Pt: Brown. 4½"

Detail in this figure is soft. Was cast in simple, two-piece mold.

**406. PIGS**
    c1910. Ger. Pt: Brown. 4"

Popular, small fun-group cast by Gladenbeck Foundry in Berlin.

**407. APPRENTICE**
    c1900. Aus. Pt: Green 6½"

Hard expression on figure's face reflects the difficult work this apprentice performs.

**408. SPILLING by M. Picciole**
    c1890. Ger. Pt: Yellow-brn. 8"

Lad with happy carefree smile fills and spills his vessel.

**409. BROKEN by L. Culuche**
    c1900. Fr. Pt: Yellow-brn. 11"

Pained expression and broken water-jug completes story about this boy with wooden shoes and patch on trousers.

**410. YOUNG FISHERMAN**
    **by Adolph-Jean Lavergne**
    c1900. Fr. Pt: Brown. 19"

Hollow-cast in nine pieces; base, arms, legs, upper and lower torso connected at waist, hat and pole. White spot is cork.

**411. NATURE BOY by Charles Lemarquier**
    1893. Fr. Pt: Gold enamel. 12"

Piece was inspired by boy found in forest raised by and living among wolves. He is shown here examining finger pricked by thorn; note his two little friends on base. This work was cast by Louchet Foundry, Paris; also in 16" edition.

**414. FEMMES FATALES by Edouard E. Drouot**
    c1900. Fr. Pt: Lt. brn. 16x27"

Foils engaged in sporting combat, these lovely young socialites are learning the "manly" art of fencing. Intricate folds and deep detail on lace of garments. Facial expressions correspond to ladies relative positions. Note grace of free arms and hands, as flashing blades and swirling skirts give motion and excitement to this study in bronze by Drouot who was one of France's most talented sculptors. His works covered a wide range of subjects—Indians, animals, mythology, and contemporary turn-of-the-century figures.

414

417

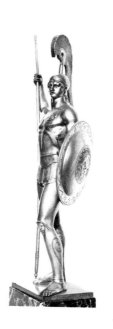

419

421

423

425

427

# L. GŌTZ.

### 417. ACHILLES by Johannes Gotz
c1900. Ger. Pt: Yellow. 18"

This powerful work, in monumental size, resides at Corfu. Thick neck and small head exaggerate proportions of figure's body. Plummage, head, and neck of swan form top of helmet. Portrait, along with snakes of Medusa, comprise design on face of shield. Gladenbeck, Berlin is founder of this small edition of "Achilles."

According to Greek mythology, Achilles was the bravest warrior in the Trojan War. Legend has it that his mother immersed him, as an infant, into the River Styx, so that he would be invulnerable in battle. The heel by which she held him remained dry, and hence, mortal. In combat, a poisoned dart, shot by Paris, pierced his heel, fatally wounding him.

### 419. ATHENA by Thiermann
c1900. Ger. Pt: Green. 12"

Thiermann's Athena is younger, prettier and more immodest than traditionally depicted; only the helmet positively identifies her. Athena was recognized by the ancient Greeks as the goddess of wisdom, arts, sciences, and "righteous" warfare.

### 421. ODYSSEUS by Huzel
c1850. Fr. Pt: Gold. 14"

Odysseus, in full armor and with spear and shield, is captured in a pensive and tranquil mood. He is the central figure in many legends, among which he is credited for being Greece's strategist in the Trojan War. He was responsible for the construction of the great Trojan Horse and hatching the plan for getting it rolled through the gates of the impenetrable walled city.

### 423. ROMAN by Kesk
c1875. Ger. Pt: Black. 13½"

Athletic-looking subject makes an interesting sculpture. Precisely what game, sport, or occupation he is about to participate in, as suggested by gadgets held in each hand, is difficult to ascertain. Strong character, evident in facial expression, indicates this man may have been an actual figure taken from history or literature.

# LCVCQVE

### 425- ROLANDO and GIL BLAS
### 427. by Edmond Louis Auguste Leveque
c1860. Fr. Pt: Grey brn. 21"

Pictured here are only two of several characters from literature sculpted by Leveque and cast by The Miroy Brothers Foundry in Paris.

Rolando de Cantarrel (425) is hero and adventurer from a Spanish romance of the early 17th century. Posed in armored vest and braced by musket, he stares into distance as if contemplating perils of a hazardous journey ahead.

Gil Blas de Santillane (427) is a romantic figure from a Spanish tale written by Le Sage in 1725. He was a vain young man, whose character improved as time went on. Gil Blas is shown here armed with hand-gun, musket, and sword; his gloved, outstretched hand contains coins from purse lying at his foot.

431

**432**

**433**

**434**

436

438

439

441

## THE SHEPHERDESS (431—434)

*The little shepherdess is universally known through nursery rhymes and countless children's tales. In art and sculpture she is generally depicted with bonnet and staff. Presented here are four interesting variations on the basic theme.*

431. SEARCHING by Paul Tillet
 c1890. Fr. Pt: Brown. 37"

This Victorian "Little Bo Peep", with delicate fingers and realistic textured complexion, is cast in two body sections. Arms and legs, cast individually, are joined at shoulders and petticoat. 18" edition was also produced.

432. BACK TO SAFETY by Jean Louis Gregoire
 c1880. Fr. Pt: Black. 21"

Shepherdess raises skirts as she carefully crosses stream to return runaway lamb to flock. Piece, on swivel base, was cast by Sussi Brothers Foundry in Paris.

433. BO PEEP LAMP BASE
 c1910. Aus. Pt: Brn. 6½" (to head)
Small Bo Peep lovingly holds lamb.

434. IL PLEUT BERGERE by Sylvain Kinsburger
 c1890. Fr. Pt: Grey. 18"

Graceful, pleasing interpretation of shepherdess. Piece has decorative plaque on second base.

## BASES

*Proper bases on pieces are important, as they can add height, improve beauty, give information, and thus, increase value.*

*Figures 438 and 439 have missing bases. A piece of marble, slightly larger in circumference than the figure itself, at the foot, would complete each.*

*Figures 432 and 441 are on swivel bases, which separate from the figure when lifted. Such bases often carry a founder's mark. Cross-bar and receptacle on underside of piece indicate there should be a swivel base.*

*Figures 434, 436 and 444 have plaques affixed to their bases. Plaques usually bear such information as title, sculptor, date, origin, exhibitions and awards.*

*Figure 431, becuase of its height, needs base to increase circumference and improve stability. And Figure 447 requires a block of proper size to add arm support.*

436. CHANT DES ALOUETTES
 by Hippolyte-Francois Moreau
 c1895. Fr. Pt: Dk. brn. 17½"

Beautiful head and tiny hand is interesting feature of "Song of the Birds." Close-up view reveals perfection of fingernails. Flair in jacket was achieved by complicated casting procedure. Arms of figure are attached at sleeves.

438. DREAMING by Auguste Moreau
 c1895. Fr. Pt: Brn. & grn. paint. 21"

Birds frolic near foot of subject, which receives some support from rake. White-metal casting, is revealed by pitting common only to this type of metal.

439. FEATHERED FRIEND by Van Der Straeten
 c1890. Fr. Pt: Brown. 15"

Hands and smile indicate delight of young lady in playing hostess to a friend. Two-sectioned torso is attached under ruffles at hips.

441. SAVED by Mathurin Moreau
 c1905. Fr. Pt: Choc. brn. 28"

Young girl comes to rescue of baby birds. Her softness contrasts pleasantly with intricate detail of branch and nest. This work also cast in smaller bronze editions and has been copied in contemporary chalk. Foundor is E. Godeau, Paris.

442. STREET SCENE
 c1910. Fr. Pt: Paint. 12"

Happy youth with bird; an appealing white-metal piece with fanciful base.

444. LA CLEF DES CHAMPS by C. Anfrie
 c1900. Fr. Pt: Grey. 17"

Fly away home! Pretty miss abets "escape" but she and bird both appear to have mixed emotions. Handle of missing cage is seen in left hand.

445. UNDECIDED by G. Wagner
 c1900. Ger. Pt: Dk. grn. 20"

Lovely nude listens to arrogant talking-frog ask for a kiss. Tiny cape and crown suggest that frog is in reality a handsome prince. Inspired by a Grimm Fairy Tale.

447. TWEET, TWEET by Moreau
 c1890. Fr. Pt: Brn-green. 16"

Charming cherub-type figure rendered in typical Moreau style.

442

444

445

447

448

449

450

451

452

453

454

455

·C· CUMBERWORTH

457

458

459

460

448. GIRLS by Karl-Joseph Werner
     c1910. Aus. Pt: Dark brn. 6½"

Two smiling young girls, glancing upwards, hold
handle of basket, which may have functioned as
cigarette container. Fused position of two figures
permits application of simple molding and casting
techniques.

449- INCROYABLE IN LOVE
450. c1900. Fr. Pt: Gold & brn. 7"

This quaint pair of figures, who seem to be over-
acting, could very well have been performing in
pantomime upon a stage. Pieces are solid cast and
each rests on a marble column.

451. LOVERS
     c1825. Fr. Pt: Natural tarnish. 5"

Young man offers rose to his lady-love. Charming
desk-size ornament is cast in sections, similar to
method used for larger-type pieces.

452. NEST by Charles Cumberworth
     c1840. Fr. Pt: Brown. 14"

Cumberworth captures the tenderness of young
love as he shows attractive maiden accepting nest
of baby birds from her youthful admirer. Piece is
cast in many sections, as revealed by maze of rods,
pins and welds on underside.

453. TOP HATS
     c1910. Aus. Pt: Red-brown. 5½"

Fashionably attired couple wear matching top hats.
The lady sports tuxedo jacket and vest over floor-
length skirt. The gentleman is dressed in checkered
trousers, vest, and long suit-coat. Figures are standing on base of pink marble.

454- PILLARS
455. c1825. Fr. or Ger. Pt: Dk. red-brn. 7"

Top half of male and female figures designed to
cleverly form matching, slim pedestals for use as
furniture supports. Pieces are solid cast and finished to perfection.

457. NICHEE by Dutrion
     c1900. Fr. Pt: Light brn & gold. 20"

Fancy-bordered bonnet frames face of lovely girl
with ornate, dangling earrings. Subject-matter, en-
chanting facial expression, and position of hands
combine to make this bust a charming work of art.

458. BOYS by Wiest (founder)
     c1850. Fr. Pt: Silver. 6½"

Boys in 17th century attire are gracefully balanced
on round base as they lift heavy receptacle. Translucent, cream-colored stone base, not shown, completes fine small sculpture.

459. JULIET OF VERONA
     by Louis-Emile-Paul Loiseau Rousseau
     c1895. Fr. Pt: Grey-brn. 17½"

Bust of woman is outstanding for detail in texture
of gown, hair, and steeple-shaped headdress. Poise,
serenity, and aloof expression indicate this is a
woman of culture and aristocratic background.

460. ANTON BRUDNER by Victor Tilgner
     1897. Aus. Pt: Brown. 11"

Portrait of an aging leader, with face showing
strength, dignity, alertness, and perceptiveness.
His casual, wrinkled attire tends to further rein-
force his inner qualities and attitudes.

461. RESTING
     c1825. Fr. Pt: Yellow. 5"

Young boy collecting berries in woods takes a
moment to rest. He is gazing at something in front
of him -- an object which appears to be missing
from sculpture. A filled-in hole, detectable only
from the underside, verifies this fact. A tiny
bronze butterfly or bird sitting on base would
complete piece.

462. BIRDS & BOY. Unsigned.
     c1825. Fr. Pt: Dk. brn. 7½"

Close examination of piece shows one bird perched
near boy's left hand and another pecking away at
wheat in basket. This early 19th century work is
example of finest quality in patina, detail, and casting technique.

463. LADY & BUTTERFLY by Gerald Gautier
     c1800. Fr. Pt: Grey. 8½"

Butterfly and right hand of figure, the focal point
of piece, are slightly out of proportion. Oval
marble base is missing, apparent by two studs protruding at bottom of figure.

464. MEOW, MEOW by Carlier
     c1890. Fr. Pt: Brown. 30"

Good composition makes this work pleasing to
view from all sides; and its message will be em-
braced by cat-lovers, who can appreciate a mother
cat's concern for her kitten. The woman shown
here offers the feline a reassuring look, while kitten
rests securely in her hand.

461

462

463

464

466

468

470

472

**466. DIANA & HOUND** by Paul Duboy
  c1870. Fr. Pt: Grey. 13"

Close positioning of figure and dog on small base lends height, slenderness, and overall elegance to this fine work. Closeup view of Diana's head shows elaborate hairdo, as well as her moon-sliver hair ornament.

**468. READING LADY** by Eutrope Bouret
  c1870. Fr. Pt: Brown. 13"

Similar in style to Duboy's "Diana" (466), but with book and narrow commode replacing arrow and hound. Here, too, tall and slimline elegance is achieved by close grouping.

# A.Ruff

**470. MOTHER'S LABOR** by Andreas Ruff
  c1910. Aus. Pt: Grn. enamel. 8"

Shawled peasant mother carries double load. The hardships of poverty are revealed on faces of both mother and child. Figures are solid cast. Fitted bronze plate covers hollow-cast base.

# PRADIER

**472. PRINCESSES LUISE & FRIEDERIKE**
  by Jean-Jacques Pradier
  c1840. Fr. Pt: Black. 11"

One of many versions of the beautiful Prussian princesses. Pradier deviates from dull composition by sculpting figures with attention focused to side and rear. Clever casting, too: base and ladies' skirts are hollow-cast in one piece to waistline; upper torsos are cast separately; and each arm is individually molded and attached at shoulder.

# CARRIER BELLEUSE

**475. FESTIVAL-BOUND**
  by Albert-Ernest Carrier Belleuse
  c1870. Fr. Pt: Yellow-brn. 27"

Dancing babes, grouped close to central female figure, artfully conceal their singular mission of enticing her to Festival of Bacchus--an orgie of fun-loving, affectionate satyrs and drunken bacchantes. This major work from fertile mind and nimble fingers of Carrier Belleuse also reflects his sense of humor, as evidenced by smaller baby-bacchus' expression as he momentarily becomes entangled in bacchante's swirling garment. Each figure, supported only by toes touching base of statue, gives "Festival-Bound" an extremely light and open appearance.

**479. L'ALLEGRO** by Jean-Louis Gregoire
  c1875. Fr. Pt: Red-brown. 36"

Bacchus-baby holds bacchic figure in one hand and small horn in other as he leads two bacchantes to the festival of wine and revelry. Tambourine and pine-cone, traditional accessories to this type of subject, are major elements in piece's overall composition. Faces of Gregoire's two female figures express both alertness and sobriety.

Although the sculptor Gregoire never achieved the fame his talent merited, he undoubtedly received ample commissions and derived much satisfaction from seeing his works cast in bronze by Sussi Brothers, one of Paris' top founders.

"L'Allegro" was also cast in a smaller 24" edition.

*L. Gregoire.*

475

479

482.  LE CONTE DE FEE by Carl Brose
      c1910.  Fr.  Pt: Light brown.  11"

Grandmother seated in large cushioned chair tells fairy-tale to her attentive grandson.  Faces are study in contrasts between youth and age.  Legs of chair, decorative upholstery fringe, and hem of old lady's dress cover specially-shaped marble slab and allows main elements to be cast as single hollow unit, except for extended arm.  Child was cast solid and is attached as separate unit.

485.  BABY WRESTLING GOOSE
      by F. Barbedienne
      c1860.  Fr.  Pt: Dk. brown.  7"

Struggle between baby-boy and large goose is mythological parody of more "Herculean" feats, a popular subject over the centuries.  This delightful work has been resculpted and cast (not recast) by Barbedienne, whose "Reduction Mecanique" seal appears under goose's tail.

488.  THREAD OF LIFE by Carrier Belleuse
      c1860.  Fr.  Pt: Lt. yellow-brn.  14"

Story in mythology, inspiration behind this piece, concerns thread of life, which is woven by one goddess, measured by another, and cut by a third.  Depicted here is the third goddess with a youth reaching out for his full measure.  Hollow-cast and chased to perfection, piece has ring and shine of fine porcelain.

489.  THE FAMILY by Clodion
      c1880.  Fr.  Pt: Black.  16"

Splendid four-figure statue by Clodion, master of mythological groupings.  Family members are closely positioned, interrelate, and form unity of direction and purpose.  Missing from piece is pine-cone, which should be attached to branch held in upraised hand of mother and child (at top of grouping).  Work also cast with oval base and in larger size.

490.  BABY PAN by Paul Silvestre
      c1920.  Fr.  Pt: Grey.  4"

Baby Pan, horns just beginning to sprout, sits cross-legged on marble base.  He is practicing and looks downward to make certain his fingers are positioned accurately on pipe.  Figure is solid cast and arms are fitted at biceps.

491.  DADDY'S HELPER by Jos.-Charles Marin
      c1800.  Fr.  Pt: Brown.  22½"

Satyr's hand forms center of arc, which encircles two heads and satyr's arm, shoulder, and raised hoof.  Scene depicts seduction of juvenile bacchante, probably attending first festival.  Festival accessories are shown scattered randomly on base.  Clever, erotic work by Marin, student and imitator of Clodion, is hollow-cast in many sections.

495.  BACCHANALIA by Claude-Michel Clodion
      c1800.  Fr.  Pt: Black-green.  22"

A masterpiece in grace and composition, grouping combines all elements of the bacchanalia: pan-pipes, pine-cones, tambourine, grapes and satyr.  Cast in fourteen segments; arms and legs are fitted and attached to torsos.  Slimmest fingers, finest faces, and satin-smooth surface are qualities which identify this piece from later recasts.  "Bacchanalia" also was cast in abbreviated version, without satyr.

**482**

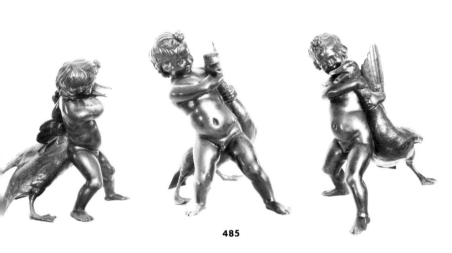

**485**

**488**

490

489        491

495

**499**

**502**

505

506

## THE ORACLE (499-506)

*The oracle, an earthly representative of its respective god on Mount Olympus, played an important role in ancient Greece. The oracle was relied on as a confidant; it could foretell the future, make demands, be offended, as well as appeased or bribed. With their multiple functions and prominence in affairs of daily living, it is not surprising that oracles were often the subject of paintings and sculptures.*

499. FIRST SECRET CONFIDENCE TO VENUS
by Francois Jouffrey
1839. Fr. Pt: Gold & brn. 25"

Young girl standing on toes whispers into ear of a passive-looking Venus. Moments earlier she had offered Venus two doves, lying on base, and a garland of flowers, draped carefully on pedestal. By baring herself of clothing, implication is she has nothing to hide; her garment can be seen hanging on back of oracle's stand.

This appealing statue has been recast in bronze, white metal and chalk, and has inspired several variations of its theme. First to edit a popular reduction of it in bronze was Barbedienne.

502. PAN AND BACCHANTE
by Hippolyte-Alexandre-Julien Moulin
c1865. Fr. Pt: Black & brn. 5"

Lovely, tiny nude bacchante gives Pan sip of wine from shell; and from all appearances, he is delighted with the attention. Pan is appropriately decorated with pan-pipes and pine-cone. Bacchante's tambourine rests against pedestal at base of figure.

*Moulin*

505. SECRET FROM ON HIGH by Moulin
1874. Fr. Pt: Green to brn. 20"

A quotation from the "Illustrated Catalog" of the Centennial International Exhibition of 1876 aptly describes this statue as follows: "The elastic pose of Mercury indicates admirably the levity of the messenger-god; it seems to be with difficulty that his figure can touch the earth. Bending gently, he confides his communication to a terminal image of a satyr, which will presently be consulted as an oracle by some credulous mortal. We can fancy the answer, quite satiric, which the grinning figure will give. The form of Mercury in this bronze is really a masterpiece of simplicity and grace."

506. CUPID—SATYR THERMOMETER.
Unsigned.
c1890. Fr. Pt: Gold. 9"

Mischievous baby-Cupid, perched on shoulders of oracle, tugs at its ears. Annoyed satyr glances back rather helplessly. Could it be that Cupid's toes are tickling it as well?

507. VICI by Auguste Moreau
c1910 Fr. Pt: Brn. enamel. 23½"

Cupid, standing on toes with legs together, poses proudly with his spread wings and bow, which cleverly manages to cover his nakedness. His expression projects the message "I came, I saw, I conquered." Figure is hollow-cast, thick and heavy, in alloy of white metals.

508. SAY PLEASE by Emile Peynot
c1885. Fr. Pt: Black. 12"

Cupid, his bow on base, vainly attempts to reach his quiver strap, which Venus teasingly holds above her head. Artful composition and balance achieved by Peynot's imaginative positioning of Venus' hands.

509. CUPID & VENUS by Duchoiselle
c1835 Fr. Pt: Dk. brown. 15"

Mother Venus appears to have situation well in hand as she reprimands Cupid for his pranks and threatens to break his newly acquired weapon. Six separate sections, visible through large opening in base, fit together to form figure of Venus.

*Duchoiselle*

507

508

509

510

512

513

517

510. LE SECRET by Etienne-Henri Dumaige
c1865. Fr. Pt: Green. 31"

Cupid as a boy, with half-grown wings, whispers to lovely, attentive maiden. What he is saying to her is their secret and is left to one's imagination. A second base of bronze, bearing the title inscription, is not shown.

*Neeb*
*Gladenbeck & S.*

512. CUPID AT HER SIDE by Neeb
c1850. Ger. Pt: Light brn. 10"

Beautiful half-nude, with garment draped around marble pillar, has winged cherub clinging to her thigh. Fingers of woman's outstretched hands are playing musical pipes, missing from bronze pictured here. Superb craftsmanship of casting, by Gladenbeck Foundry in Berlin.

513. LOVE ON BOOKS
c1825. Fr. Pt: Natural yellow. 7½"

Top of vase opens into inkwell. Base and figure are hollow-cast, paper-thin, in one piece. Arms, wings, vase, and ornate legs of base are attached separately.

517. CUPID AND PSYCHE
by Albert-Ernest Carrier-Belleuse
c1865. Fr. Pt: Brown. 18"

Psyche, curiosity getting the best of her, holds lamp over her lover's face to see who it is that comes to her only in the dark of night. Cupid, awakened by a drop of hot oil, is saddened by sight of Psyche doing the forbidden--looking upon a god. "Love cannot dwell where there is no trust," he declares, and flies away, wounded. The repentant Psyche is finally forgiven, however, after many trials, arranged by Venus, to test her love for Cupid. The god of love returns to fly her back with him to Mt. Olympus, where she would be made immortal and they could then be married.

Mounted on its original stepped, marble base, this sculpture is a rare and intriguing piece.

*Dumaige*

519. LEDA AND THE SWAN by Louis Kley
c1875. Fr. Pt: Dk. brn. 16½"

Sculptor's interpretation of mythological tale in which Zeus falls in love with Leda, a mortal. To avoid being discovered by his wife Hera, Zeus visits and seduces Leda in the form of a dazzling white swan. Kley's "Leda And The Swan" is a mildly erotic work on this popular theme.

## THE JUDGMENT OF PARIS (520 & 522)

*Paris, banished prince of Troy, holds the "Apple of Discord," which is inscribed with the message, "For the fairest." According to Greek mythology, Paris was ordered by Zeus to pass judgment on this matter. Paris chose Aphrodite, who promised to give him Helen, the most beautiful woman in the world. The goddess arranged for their meeting, and Paris whisked Helen away to Troy, an act which precipitated the Greek-Trojan War. This moment of decision, or "judgment," is regarded as the most important single incident in all mythology and has become the subject of numerous sculptures.*

520. PARIS by Emile-Francois Fouquet
c1850. Fr. Pt: Brown. 11½"

521. GREEK by F. Barbedienne (foundry)
c1860. Fr. Pt: Brown. 5"

522. PARIS ON SPHINX by Eusele
1850. Fr. Pt: Brown. 11"

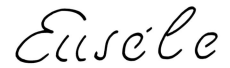

519

520

521

522

524

528

532

535

**524. MANDOLIN PLAYER** by Emile Laporte
c1885. Fr. Pt: Black. 21"

Simple, well done decorative figure of young
lady as she plucks the strings of her mandolin.

**528. CHANTEUR FLORENTINE** by Paul Dubois
1865. Fr. Pt: Brown. 24"

Period-style clothing gives young singer an almost
nude look. He sings a tune while nonchantly
strumming on mandolin; eight pegs on instrument
are made so they actually turn. Figure's shoes
extend one-half inch below base, where they are
fitted and bolted to receptacles. Later editions
of this work have soles of shoes screwed to base
and fused pegs.

"Florentine Singer" was originally cast and signed
by F. Barbedienne (1865-1875); also produced in
a larger edition. Won Medal of Honor in Paris
Salon, 1865, and when displayed in Luxembourg
Gallery, Paris, became one of Europe's most popular statuettes.

**532. JEUNE PECHEUR DANSANT**
by Francisque-Joseph Duret
1833. Fr. Pt: Brown. 17"

Happy young fisherman dances spritely on toes
of one foot. Legs fitted at shorts; arms fitted
below shoulder. Torso is hollow-cast and pinned
to anchor appendages. Two closeup views of
face (at bottom of page) are dissimilar because
figures were cast by different foundries, resulting
in inevitable variations in features and detailing.

Duret's popular fisherman was done in several
editions during the 19th century. Usually they
were cast from original resculptures and, therefore, should not be regarded as recasts; finest of
these editions will have hands open and fingers
free, as in the early work pictured here.

**535. JOYEUR DE VIELLE**
by Jean-Didier Debut
c1865. Fr. Pt: Brown. 26"

Young player of Vielle (hurdy-gurdy) also sings
and dances for a few coins from an appreciative
audience. Boxed instrument he carries operates
by turning crank attached to resinous wheel
which, in turn, scrapes strings to produce sound.
Small base, only 4½" in diameter, supports subject who is balanced by toes of one foot. Figure
also cast in half-size edition.

**536. TAMBOURINE** by Hippolyte Moreau
c1900. Fr. Pt: Brn. & grn. paint. 14"

One hand of dancer rattles tambourine while
other holds end of sash. "Tambourine" is white-
metal casting, as revealed by examining underside.

**537. SPANISH DANCER** by Agathon Leonard
c1900. Fr. Pt: Gold dore. 11½"

Following the Flamenco rhythm of this dancer,
one can almost hear the castanettes click as her
skirt swirls from side to side and tassles on vest
sway with motion of her body.

**539. DECO HARLEQUIN** by A. Titze
1923. Aus. Pt: Yellow, brn.& silver. 11"

Lady harlequin with slap-stick and diamond-pat-
terned slacks retains identifying costume of her
male counterpart, while adding feminine touch of
ruffles and high-heeled shoes. Lifelike, pleasantly
smiling face enhances appeal of this solid cast
figure shown dancing on polished slate base.

**540. PRECISION DANCERS** by Kruse
c1920. Ger. Pt: Grn. & brn. 12"

Stern expressions contrast sharply with graceful
movement of two figures. Identical tilt to bodies
and position of legs indicate long hours of practice and a long-time association between these
two dancers.

**541. HAREM DANCER**
by Theodor-Karl Eichler
c1920. Ger. Pt: Paint & lacquer. 7"

Feeling of motion and excitement conveyed by
dancer's costume, gestures, and facial expression.
Smooth, quality chasing of figure. Eichler also
modeled porcelain dancers for Meissen.

**536**

**537**

**539**

**540**

**541**

**542**

BARDE
*PAR DEBUT*
2<sup>E</sup> GRAND PRIX DE
ROME

**543**

545

546

547

MOZART

548

550

552

# DE BUT

**542. BARDE by Jean-Didier Debut**
   1851. Fr. Pt: Brn. & gold. 20½"
Sword, medallion, feathered hat, and flowing sleeves all add decorative touch to figure of bearded, singing barde. This work won Second Grand Prize of Rome in 1851.

# HEINGLE

**543. LA SERENADE by Anton Heingle**
   1898. Fr. Pt: Dark green. 23½"
Sensitive-featured minstrel, with textured hat and ornate Spanish costume, plays tune on small, peg-less stylized mandolin. Lower base carries plaque from 1898 Exposition.

# L. Grégoire

**545. MOZART by Jean-Louis Gregoire**
   c1875. Fr. Pt: Dk. brn. 14"
A striking study of the boy Mozart, in attire and hair-style of his day, as he concentrates upon tuning his violin. Music-sheets lay at his feet.

**546. DANCERS**
   c1900. Aus. Pt: Yellow. 2½"
Couple waltzing along in step with music. Figures are well-detailed, considering their small size; base is no larger than a half-dollar.

**547. CELLO**
   c1900. Fr. Pt: Brn. & yellow. 8"
Lady with cello rests for moment in Art Nouveau-design chair. Unusually high back of chair adds interest to basic composition of this symbolic piece.

**548. CANDLEHOLDER by Tiffany & Co. Studios**
   c1900. Amer. Pt: Gold dore. 8"
Double candle-pots are supported in fanciful Art Nouveau holder with fleur-de-lis shaped base. Snuffer (usually missing) is hooked to extension at top of handle.

**550. MANDOLIN PLAYER**
   by Emile-Coriolan Guillemin
   c1880. Fr. Pt: Acid & paint. 22"
Gypsy-type mandolin player, in Arabic costume, is artfully rendered and produced in finest quality bronze. Figure is hollow-cast, very thin.

Ladies in Guillemin's sculptures are extremely lifelike, with much of the credit going to his founder who, by never marking his works, remains unidentified.

**552. SITA by Guillemin**
   c1880. Fr. Pt: Acid & paint. 32"
Dark-skinned Sita, an Arab dancing girl, was sculpted from same model as Fig. 550. Left foot of figure extends off base, with right foot positioned to give piece proper balance. Title of sculpture appears under slipper.

554

555

556

557

558

560

### 554. FLOREAL by Emile Pinedo
1893. Fr. Pt: Choc. brn. 20"

Bust, exhibited in Columbian Exposition (Chicago 1893), has seal of Pinedo Studio and a "Bronze Garanti" seal. Textured pedestal, hat, and blouse contrast with glass-like complexion. Hat and plaque are attached separately. Red marble base matches and complements shape of pedestal.

### 555. NATURE BOY by Alfred-Jos. Charron
c1895. Fr. Pt: Dk. brn. 9½"

Popularized boy of the forest, reared and living among wolves, portrayed by Charron as free and happy. Shoulders and chest of youth meld into tall bronze stalk, which rests on circular slab of red marble.

### 556. LA VIENE by Besserdigi
c1905. Aus. Pt: Brown. 3"

Deluxe miniature souvenir bust, solid cast on decorative Art Nouveau hollow base. Fitted bronze plate seals base, adding touch of elegance.

### 557. SOUVIENS TOI by Andreas Ruff
c1905. Aus. Pt: Brown. 3"

Deluxe, miniature souvenir bust, solid cast on decorative Art Nouveau hollow base. Fitted bronze plate seals base, adding touch of elegance.

### 558. ROBIN HOOD by Victor Auririedria
c1915. Amer. Pt: Brown. 8"

Much hand-finishing on face of smiling youth with Robin Hood cap. Bust was signed on backside of clay original.

### 560. LA PARISIENNE by Jean-Louis Gregoire
c 1880. Fr. Pt: Black. 20"

Fine piece with satin-like finish was cast by Sussi Brother, Paris. Magnificent detail is rendered by Gregoire in study of beautiful young lady clothed in most fashionable attire of her time.

### 561. ALMEE by Emmanuele Villanis
c1890. Fr. Pt: Grn. & brn. paint. 7"

White-metal bust of provocative Arabian maiden. Head is typically Villanis, but arms and base design are unique to his style.

### 562. ALICE by Buice
c1870. Fr. Pt: Brown. 17"

Simplicity of base and dress is designed to draw attention to woman's face, which captures a quality of character reflecting directness and sincerity.

### 563. BUSTY
c1900. Aus. Pt: Dk. brown. 2½"

Miniature bronze, with over-emphasized bosom, has surprisingly well done face and hair detail.

### 564. BLOSSOM by Rudolph Miro
c1870. Ger. Pt: Silver wash. 2½"

Small bust captures personality of figure with blossoms in hair and on chest. Piece rests on miniature base of red marble.

### 566. JOAN OF ARC by Raoul Larche
c1895. Fr. Pt: Yellow & brn. 12"

Popular version of Joan cast by Siot Decauville. Original edition was numbered; recasts are unmarked and do not have opening in fall of hair over figure's right shoulder-blade (see inset).

### 567. NYMPHE by Emmanuele Villanis
c1900. Fr. Pt: Green & brn. 5"

Bust of beautiful young woman, in white metal on marble base, by the master of goddess-like faces.

561

562

563

564

566

567

569

570

573

574

581

575

576

577

### BOY'S BEST FRIEND (569 & 573)

*Young boy and his dog was a favorite subject of yesteryear, just as it is today. Two competing, award-winning works on this theme--Figures 569 and 573--were exhibited at Paris Salon of 1882 and are shown here in their original bronze editions by Sussi Brothers.*

569. **UN FUTUR ARTISTE**
by Henri-Honore Ple
1882. Fr. Pt: Brown. 16"

From the time of Ple's debut, in 1877, until the turn-of-the-century, works of this talented sculptor won many coveted awards. Among his successes are: Slave Girl, Echo, Joan of Arc, Aphrodite, Spring, and Harvest.

570. **BUSTER BROWN** by Carl Kauba
c1910. Ger. Gold & brn. 6"

Comic-strip character and his mischievous dog, as rendered by Kauba, sculptor renown for his prolific and versatile works.

573. **FRIENDS** by Eugene-Antoine Aizelin
1882. Fr. Pt: Dk. brn. 16"

Aizelin's long and fruitful career spanned 50 years--from his debut, in 1852, till his death in 1902. He is recognized for his operatic, biblical, and mythological subjects.

574. **DUTCH BOY**
c1920. Amer. Pt: Dk. brn. 8"

Well-defined figure has simulated double base formed as part of bust. Heavy copper electroplating over unglazed porcelain and an acid patina make "Dutch Boy" difficult to distinguish from solid bronze.

575. **PAX**
c1910. Fr. Pt: Brown. 4"

Bust, in white metal, was upper part of clockcase. Its design is blend of New and Deco art.

576. **LILIO**
c1900. Fr. Pt: Grn. & brn. 4"

Excellent quality souvenir Art Nouveau miniature bust has fitted bronze plate covering bottom.

577. **LADY** by A. Zielbauer
c1900. Ger. Pt: Brown. 4½"

Portrait of lady exhibits fine face, expressive eyes and simple hairdo. Bust sits on contoured, red marble base.

581. **LE CAIRE** by Charles-Henri-Joseph Cordier
1866. Fr. Pt: Brn. & bronze. 15"

Egyptian lady with majestic expression has earrings of semi-precious stones, ornate jewelry and headdress, and long braids hanging down back. Cordier traveled to the far corners of the earth sculpting the dress and mood of its people.

582. **PRINCESS LOINTAINE** by Marius Vallet
1895. Fr. Pt: Brn. & gold. 21"

Sarah Bernhardt, renown French actress--and patron of the Art Nouveau movement--depicted here as Princess Lointaine, heroine in Rostand's drama. Figure cast by Decauville of Paris.

584. **STEPPING** by Marius Vallet
c1900. Fr. Pt: Grn. & brn. 10"

Graceful, fairy-like figure, with aloof expression and Art Nouveau hairstyle, is solid cast and has bronze hollow base.

586. **FLOREAL** by Causse Cadet
c1900. Fr. Pt: Grn. & brn. paint. 25"

High Art Nouveau styling is evident in figure's gown, hair, flowers and base all flowing into one another. "Floreal," Mother Nature's beautiful dreaming flower, is cast in silver-blue zinc (white metal).

587. **NOUVEAU LADY.** Unsigned.
c1900. Fr. Pt: Silver & brn. paint. 10"

Decorative white-metal figure is designed in typical Art Nouveau fashion; lady's gown swirls to below knees and then fans out to form base of sculpture.

133

582

584

586

587

589

590

592

593

## MOVEABLE BRONZES (589 & 227, 664, 665)

*The term "moveable bronzes" applies to a special category of small, erotic, imaginative "trick" pieces. They are rare and highly prized specialty items of Austrian origin.*

*The outer shell, or wrap, of these pieces may be in the form of a bear, frog, rat, alligator, dragon, devil, castle, tent, box, rock, or sphinx, to mention a few of their many shapes. They open by spring-action, at the touch of a button, or by a camouflaged triggering device activated, for example, by turning a shoe, pulling a tail, or lifting an arm. Inside the shell there is a tiny, golden provocative nude, who may be either standing, sitting, crouching, or reclining.*

*Among the rare and more ingenius moveable bronzes are those with clock-type movements. The mechanism allows the figure to change position or open slowly. A woman's hands, for example, may rise slowly to cover her eyes as her gown is removed; a fur coat and muff may open, leaving the lady bare; or, doors may swing open as a nude turns or rolls over.*

### 589. DISROBED
c1900. Aus. Pt: Gold & grn. paint. 7"

Stretching lady, clad in full length robe, is unveiled by flick of her buckle. Closing hinged robe cocks the springs and figure is again ready to perform.

### 590. DRAPED by Van de Vin
c1900. Fr. Pt: Yellow. 11"

Delicate hollow casting from base to upper hand makes this piece very light in weight. Very well done work, with focal point formed by draping of woman's garment, a seamless sheet of cloth.

### 592. SLEEPY by Gustav Gurschner
c1900. Aus. Pt: Grn. & brn. 7½"

Unique candle-holder and lady, rendered in "slimline" New Art fashion. Its sculptor, Gurschner, was noted for early electric lamp designs, candlesticks, ashtrays and inkwells which used tall, slim Viennese women as their central theme.

### 593. DOOR GUARD
c1900. Fr. Pt: Brown. 22"

Heavy, Art Nouveau-styled door guard cast in New York by Tiffany. Period fixtures such as these may still be found mounted in their original installation.

### 594. DANCER by More
c1910. Ger. Pt: Yellow-brn. 8"

Smooth skin chasing and textured surface of clothing combine to make "Dancer" an appealing work.

### 595. NUDE ON VASE by Carl Kauba
c1905. Ger. Pt: Lt. & dk. bronze. 10"

Smooth finish of young nude, cast as part of vase, contrasts markedly with form and texture of vase. Fine example of Kauba's imaginative designs and versatility.

### 596. CAVALIER by Emmanuel Fremiet
c1870. Fr. Pt: Gold. 12"

Sixteenth century cavalier, with sword, cape and plumed hat, strikes a typical pose. Fremiet, one of France's most acclaimed sculptors of the period, also did mythological subjects, equestrian themes, and animals (of quality equal to Barye's).

### 597. BACCHANTE AT PILLAR
c1840. Fr. Pt: Brown. 10"

Old bronze, unsigned, with separately cast pillar and figure. At one time possessed marble base or was used to decorate top of a clock.

### 599. THE CIGARETTE by M. Fiorucci
c1925. Origin unknown. Pt: Dk. brn.
Ht: 8" Length: 14"

Study of nude, in early Art Deco styling, presented in rather novel manner.

594

595

596

597

599

**601**

AU CLAIR DE LA LUNE

**602**

604

607

601. AU CLAIR DE LA LUNE
by Eutrope Bouret
c1875. Fr. Pt: Dk. brn. 18"

Bouret's popular pierrot, sadly serenading the moon, was cast in larger and smaller editions, in various patinas, and with assorted bases. Pierrot, a character and stock figure in French pantomime, had whitened face, loose pantaloons, and jacket with large buttons.

602. PIERROT by E. Wante
c1910. Fr. Pt: Gold enamel. 16"

Garbed in typical pierrot costume, character is sculpted as he engages in encounter with stubborn bird perched on fence.

604. JUGGLER by Emile Henri LaPorte
c1890. Fr. Pt: Dk. brn. 12½"

Entertainer, clad in skin-tight costume with butterfly design, gracefully performs his act. He stands on base styled to resemble wooden platform.

*G de Chemellier*

607. GET UP! by George de Chemillier
1884. Fr. Pt: Dk. brn. 24"

Clown-trainer with unicorn hair-cap snaps his fingers to ready his dog for jump through hoop. Graceful turn of figure and pulling of fabric on tights is excellent. Figure was also cast in smaller edition.

608. GYPSY by C. F. Sornin
c1870. Fr. Pt: Brown. 28"

Bow on finger of extended hand indicates reason for beautiful gypsy girls's languished expression. Antique red marble base completes piece.

609. YARN by Eutrope Bouret
c1870. Fr. Pt: Brown. 12½"

Graceful, early work was probably top on fine clock. Beautiful detail, particularly in natural folds and draping of Grecian-style garment.

*Bouret.*

611. WISHING by Hella Unger
c1900. Ger. Pt: Light brn. 11"

Formation of rocks and water makes unusual base for figure to perch on. Young lady, standing with hands behind her, presents a slim, exaggerated, silhouette.

612. GRAPES by Clodion
c1850. Fr. Pt: Dk. grn. 13"

Position of arms and legs lend interest to this composition and gives it a sense of movement. Cymbals and grapes are evidence of figure's role as bacchante.

613. THE MESSAGE
c1850. Fr. Pt: Yellow. 12"

Grecian lady, supported by pillar, appears delighted by message on scrolled note she is holding.

615. SHEPHERDS by Toblueigrth
c1900. Ger. Pt: Lt. brn. 13"

Fusion of legs, arms and bodies gives figure a pleasing compactness. Softness of detail is by intent, and should not be mistaken for poor molding.

616. PHEASANT by R. P. Bergman
c1900. Ger. Pt: Brown. 9½"

Proud, bearded hunter examines his prize. Figure originally held gun in left hand. Treatment of subject, casting and finishing similar to Kauba's, but on quality-scale would rate one notch below.

617. RACKET
c1900. Aus. Pt: Lt. brown. 3"

Fashionably dressed gentleman is solid cast in one piece. Fine features, considering tiny size of head.

618. DUTCH BOY
c1900. Aus. Pt: Painted. 3½"

Fair quality, but highly collectible miniature. Its shape permits use of simple mold. Recasts have been produced.

616

617

618

619

620

622

LE
COUVRE-FEU

624

629

CCeribelli

634

**619. SITTING**
    c1910. Aus. Pt: Painted. 2"

Excellent quality figure, originally on marble ash-tray. Semi-free arms and bent knees make casting of this piece relatively expensive, and not the kind to be selected for recasting.

**620. SMOKING by Bergman**
    c1910. Aus. Pt: Painted. 2"

This miniature, with simple compact shape, except for extending hand, is from original edition. Paint patina fails to hide lack of detail or finishing on modern recasts.

*E. Marioton*

**622. LE COUVRE FEU by Eugene Marioton**
    c1900. Fr. Pt: Grey brn. 23"

"Cover the fire," title of this work, is an ancient term referring to town regulations that set a time when lights must be doused; Marioton captures mood of handsome lad in street as he heralds the curfew.

*Peynot*

**624. CHIMNEY SWEEP by Emile Peynot**
    c1880. Fr. Pt: Green-black. 27"

Realistically rendered figure of young chimney sweep, with scraper in one hand and gourde canteen in other, as he calls to someone below in street. Dark patina emphasizes theme of piece.

Peynot had a long and successful career as a sculptor. His exhibitions in France and Italy won him many awards and titles. His monuments appear in public places throughout Europe; and some of these sculptures were produced in reduced size for popular editions. Peynot's most popular works, however, were his representations of characters from L'Opera Comique de Paris.

**629. LES ROSES by Cesar Ceribelli**
    1907. Fr. Pt: Dull brn. 30"

Fashionably attired young lady sculpted in detailed perfection, from intricate feathers in her hat to fallen rose at her foot. Necklaces indicate she was a lady of some means.

*J. Scotte*

**634. L'AGE D'OR by T. Scotte**
    c1903. Amer. Pt: Gold. 29"

Face and figure are those of Evelyn Nesbit (Thaw), Charles Dana Gibson's favorite model. Art Nouveau styling is most evident when piece is viewed from back. Flimsy wrap on lady covers but does not conceal perfection of her form. Edition cast by Tiffany & Company, New York.

**635- L'HIVER & L'AUTOMNE**
**636.** by Hipployte-Francois Moreau
    1889. Ft. Pt: Brown. 19"

"Winter" and "Autumn", two of four female figures representing the seasons, are cast solid in several sections and have plaque on second bronze base. They were edited by Societe des Bronzes (Paris) and exhibited in Salon des Beau Arts.

**637. GLANEUSE by Henri Godet**
    1896. Fr. Pt: Dk. brn. 9"

Task of the gleaner is to collect scraps of grain left by reapers. Leaning on her rake, gleaner enjoys a moment of relaxation. Base is incised with the words "Salon des Beau Arts" and carries bronze seal of guarantee.

**640. ABUNDANCE by Eutrope Bouret**
    c1880. Fr. Pt: Yellow-brn. 16"

Young Eastern lady at harvest is symbolically posed, with wheat in arm, in hand, and at feet. Detail, such as hair, headdress and garment folds, are skillfully rendered. Work is solid cast, with its several sections pinned together.

635

636

640

637

641

642

644

CHIEN de St BERNARD

645 646

649

650

648

641. CHIHAUHAU by Jules Moigniez
c1885. Fr. Pt: Dk. brn. 8"

This small but incredibly bold dog, named for city in Mexico, originally worked for the Indians, and probably was known to the Aztecs. Study of resting Chihauhau is presented with fine detail.

642. HOUND by C. B. Dale Co.
1888. Eng. Pt: Black enamel. 13"

Exceedingly fine iron dog is solid cast, with front legs welded to body and hind feet cast as part of base. Underside of base is incised with complete registry information--country of origin, factory, material, and date of casting.

644. CHIEN DU ST. BERNARD
by Adrien-Etienne Gaudez
c1885. Fr. Pt: Brown. 17"

St. Bernard, popular dog of the 19th century, was bred by monks for intelligence, bravery and power; Gaudez's work captures these traits. Dog is sculpted returning from mission of finding young traveler lost on mountain trail.

645. FREDERICK THE GREAT
by Rudolf Kaesbach
c1900. Ger. Pt: Black. 15"

Frederick II of Prussia and his two graceful hounds are contained on octagon base with matching marble. This work often found with dogs intentionally removed, for resale as individual pieces; their absence is difficult to detect.

646. VAN DYCK by Jean-Jules Salmson
c1865. Fr. Pt: Brown. 22"

Anthony Van Dyck (1599-1641), Flemish portrait and religious painter, presents a handsome figure in his high boots, broad-brimmed hat, stylish costume, and finely trimmed moustache and beard (Van Dyck). Simple, circular base enhances elegance of this dashing character.

648. PAUL AND VIRGINIA
by Paul-Eugene Mengin
c1890. Fr. Pt: Brown. 23"

Sibling love is depicted most admirably by Mengin in his interpretation of a children's tale, by Bernardin de St. Pierre, popular in the last century. Story tells of Paul and Virginia lost in the woods; when they come upon a stream, Paul reassures his frightened sister, places her on his back, and confidently proceeds to cross it. Original edition has founder's seal.

649. FRIMAS by Suan Ferville
c1890. Fr. Pt: Grn. & brn. enamel. 14"

Shivering maiden, standing with stack of firewood, appears ill-prepared for cold wind as it whips her thin dress and chills her hands. Texture of skin, dress and wood are excellent, as is patina that covers this white-metal casting.

650. CONSOLATION by Hippolyte Moreau
c1895. Fr. Pt: Grey-black. 12"

Younger girl has been gathering flowers. She is seen with arm raised to ward off a bee as she seeks the protection of her sister. Girls' blowing garments, with their meticulously sculpted folds, give not only fabric but entire piece a look of realism.

651

652

653

655

656

658

**651. BACCHUS** by Marcus Fritzsche
c1850. Ger. Pt: Black. 27"

Grinning god of wine and revelry, Bacchus, snaps his fingers and proposes toast to "wine, women and song." In Greek mythology, he is named Dionysus.

**652-** **PAN & BACCHUS** by Schaffert
**653.** c1850. Ger. Pt: Black. 9"

Pan (652) dances along to tune he plays on long, thin pipes, missing from this statue. Tiny goat horns, identifying feature of this lesser deity and Bacchanalia participant, can be seen protruding from his head.

Bacchus (653) holds chalice in one hand and empty pitcher in other as he offers toast to Jupiter. Strapped to sling, and hanging on backside, are a tambourine and fur.

**655. BACCHUS** by Eugene-Desire Piron
1903. Fr. Pt: Dark green. 11"

Bacchus, with strong handsome features, marches to beat of his clashing cymbals. Figure took honors at 1903 Paris Salon.

**656. CAUGHT IN THE VINE**
by Clement-Leopold Steiner
1887. Fr. Pt: Dk. brn. 25"

Hercules rescues Baby Pan, whose goat legs and hoofs become tangled in vine. Statue presents interesting parody on Hercules' twelve labors; it was Gold Medal winner in 1891 Salon. Special Thiebaut Brothers seal is incised on base.

**658. BACCHANALIA BABIES** by Pradier
1834. Fr. Pt: Grn. & gold. 11"

Baby Bacchus, Pan and satyr romp with leopard, special animal of the bacchanalia. Grouping is hollow cast as a single form through a complicated procedure. Bronze ring, attached, forms second base.

**659. MARKET BOY** by Nam Greb
c1910. Aus. Pt: Multi-color paint. 3½"

African boy patiently waits for customer, so that he may serve his hot beverage. Each piece in this work, including carpet, is solid cast in bronze.

**660. WATER CARRIER**
c1900. Aus. Pt: Multi-color paint. 4½"

Good detail in lightly clad figure of Negress and the large water jugs she carries.

**661. VASE CARRIER**
c1910. Aus. Pt: Brown. 6"

Thin, hollow vase held by boy is removeable. Entire piece is rendered in fine detail.

**662. RECLINING HAREM GIRL**
c1900. Aus. Pt: Multi-color paint.
Ht: 1½" Length: 5"

Stock miniature figures, like this reclining temptress, were used to adorn ashtrays, inkwells and bronze boxes.

**664. GUARDED HAREM LAMP** by Nam Greb
c1910. Aus. Pt: Multi-color paint. 13"

Light in dome, shining through openings covered by red glass, illuminates figures. Provocatively posed harem girl and stern-looking guard, separated by curtain, rotate on turntable. This highly prized lamp is in the "moveable bronze" category of collecting.

**665. PEEPING ALI LAMP**
c1910. Aus. Pt: Multi-color paint. 13"

Hidden button activates sliding curtain, which when opened, reveals tiny golden nude. Bulb in dome throws light on the subject.

659

660

661

662

664

665

668

TRIBOULET

669

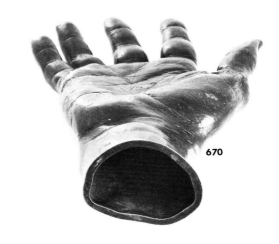

670

671    672

## 668. TRIBOULET
c1880. Fr. Pt: Brown. 13"

Court jester Triboulet (Rigoletto in Italian) is captured in moment of deep thought; perhaps, as in Verdi's opera, he is planning how to best protect his beautiful daughter from a lecherous baron.

## 669. SHOEMAKER
c1900. Aus. Pt: Multi-color paint. 3½"

Shoemaker at his work-bench, engrossed in smoking his pipe and reading a missile, is unaware of small rodent perched on boot extractor. This miniature bronze is composed of more than 40 tiny perfectly crafted pieces, all welded together.

## 670. HAND
c1900. Ger. Pt: Dk. brn. 13"

Bigger than life casting accurately duplicates every line and wrinkle, including finger-prints, contained in an adult's palm and hand. Realistic, and certainly unusual, "Hand" provokes a variety of emotions and reactions from viewer--revulsion, fear, amusement, curiosity, etc.

## 671- FLOWER VASES
## 672. c1900. Aus. Pt: Subtle trans. colors. 4½"

Miniature vases, elegantly crafted in low relief, contain female figures in garden setting.

## DAVID

*David, second king of Israel, was a most beloved and heroic figure in ancient Jewish history. He possessed the combined talents of poet, musician (harp), and warrior. His vast accomplishments overruled his human shortcomings. According to Jewish teachings, the Messiah is to be a descendant of the House of David.*

*Best known story of David, the youth, concerns his battle with Goliath, the Philistine giant. Victor, symbolically, determined the victorious army. The contest was one of skilled missile warfare (sling) versus brute force (sword). Goliath was felled by David's first stone, which found its mark to the giant's forehead. Stunned by the sudden loss of their champion, the Philistines fled, with the army of Saul in pursuit.*

## 675. DAVID by Adrien-Etienne Gaudez
1870. Fr. Pt: Choc. brn. 26"

From a distance, David prudently appraises his bragging opponent, as the two opposing armies look on. His foot, poised on rock formation, enhances composition and adds to David's look of strength and confidence. His ammunition of smooth pebbles are visible in loin cloth. Beautiful skin texture was achieved by a laborious hand-knurling technique. Figure is mounted on swivel for better viewing.

## 679. DAVID VAINQUEUR
by Marius-Jean-Antonin Mercie
1870. Fr. Pt: Trans. lt. brn. 29"

After dispatching Goliath with sling and stone, David approached the fallen giant, unsheathed his sword, and severed his head. The victor, as sculpted here, has one foot on Goliath's gaping head wound while resheathing sword. Calm, handsome face of David contrasts markedly with bearded, hairy head of Goliath.

"David Vainqueur," with its youthful lithe figure originally sculpted nude, won first prize in Rome, in 1870. Barbedienne clothed this popular work and then cast it in five sizes -- two smaller and two larger than the one shown here.

Mercie was one of the finest sculptors of the last century, and David was one of his finest works.

675

679

686

←686

687

## JUDITH

*Judith is the Jewess heroine from a book of Apocrypha. Briefly, the story relates that when General Holofernes' army invaded Palestine, and the fortress city of Bethulia was about to fall, Judith, a beautiful and stately widow, appears at the invader's camp. Attracted by her courage and charm, Holofernes invites Judith to remain with him. One evening before the imminent battle, while he lies in a drunken sleep, Judith beheads the general. With Holofernes' head hidden in a bag, she passes through the enemy lines and returns to her people. Elated by Judith's feat, the Jewish defenders were inspired to rout the foe, who had lost their leader and the will to fight.*

686. JUDITH by Guillemin
     c1880. Fr. 40"
     Pt: Acid--subtle shades of brown & red

An example of the ultimate in realism, achieved by several late 19th century French bronziers, is evident from this presentation of Guillemin's "Judith." Lifelike quality of skin is attained by special knurling technique. Figure is cast hollow, by use of close-fitting core. Semi-finished inside surface is visible through large opening in base.

687. JUDITH by Mercie
     1880. Fr. Pt: Brown. 16"

Mercie creates a masterful illusion in bronze by veiling Judith's head and face, thereby muting her headdress and features yet maintaining a clearly expressive facial posture and mood. Bronze base is complemented by red marble second base. "Judith" was edited by Goupil & Cie.

688. SHEPHERD by Charles Korschann
     c1900. Czech. Pt: Lt. brn. 12"

Five sheep, partially fused, are cast hollow, in one piece. Shepherd, solid cast, is attached.

689. DUTCH GIRL & BOWL
     c1900. Aus. Pt: Grn. & brn. 7"

Dutch water girl with vessels rests alongside large bowl, which is attached.

690. LETZTES AUFGEBOT by Beck
     1914. Ger. Pt: Brown. 8"

"Call to Duty," a German patriotic bronze, was cast at start of World War I. Cannon and broken wheel, symbolic elements, lie at foot of figure.

691. LITTLE LADY
     c1900. Aus. Pt: Yellow. 5"

Interesting design and good finish on small turn-of-the-century figure solid cast from simple mold.

692. ALAIN CHARTIER
     by Alphonse-Emmanuel de Moncel
     1894. Fr. Pt: Dk. brn. 28½"

Alain Chartier (1390-1430), French ambassador, poet and political writer, was referred to by his contemporaries as "Father of French Eloquence" and "Seneca of France." Much of his prose exposed corruption of the French court and appealed for reform and unity. Legend has it that Princess Margaret of Scotland once came upon him sleeping in a garden, and though it was said he was "the ugliest man in France," she bent down and kissed his lips because, she declared, "from that precious mouth had issued so many fair and virtuous words."

Moncel's work of Chartier, attired in period costume, aptly captures the man and the legend. Cast by R. Cottin, Paris.

688

689

690

691

692

ALAIN CHARTIER

688-A

693

697

698

# Fcois. Roger.

### 693. ACQUIS by Francois Roger
1889. Fr. Pt: Choc. brn. 25"

Happy lad of the street bounces ball, then "acquis!" --he "secures" it on rod held in one hand. With no assist from other hand allowed, game requires great concentration and skill. Smaller edition of figure, minus base plaque (see Fig. 402), was available to public at Universal Exposition 1889.

### 697. BEAUTY AT FOUNTAIN
by Gladenbeck & Sohn
c1890. Ger. Pt: Gold wash. 8"

Lovely golden lady with urn perches daintily on side of dark green marble bowl inlaid with bronze ring. Bowl is supported by four bronze pillars anchored to three-layered marble base. Lady's hand rests on side of fountain while foot and gown touch base. Elegant table centerpiece.

# Chas. Knight

### 698. ELEPHANT BOOK-END
by Charles Robert Knight
c1900. Amer. Pt: Blac,. 5"

Powerful elephant, attacking with head down, attempts to topple heavy fence. Piece is solid cast and has lead-weighted base. Knight, Brooklyn-born animalier, is noted for his savage and zoological subjects.

## MIGNON

*"Mignon," an opera by Ambroise Thomas, was first produced in Paris, Nov. 17, 1866. The main character, Mignon, is a beautiful young maiden kidnapped in childhood from her father's castle by wandering gypsies. The story begins with the gypsies whipping Mignon because she refuses to dance and play her mandolin for two strangers. The two men restrain the gypsies and, in gratitude, Mignon presents each with flowers divided equally from a bouquet. The strangers, a demented old man and a rich young student, are so touched by this action that they purchase her freedom from her captives.*

*The last scene in the opera's involved plot takes place in an old abandoned castle, which the student intends buying and living in "happily ever after" with Mignon. The old man, in the meantime, gradually regains his memory and recalls that this was the very castle he had left years ago in search of his daughter. Mignon, in turn, recollects the great halls and gardens as being those she had played in as a child. Mignon, her father, and her young lover all embrace, thus concluding the opera "Mignon" on a happy note.*

*The story of Mignon is a popular subject in art and sculpture, with Mignon usually portrayed as a beautiful shy maiden holding a mandolin or a bouquet of flowers.*

### 701. MIGNON by Hippolyte-Francois Moreau
c1900. Fr. Pt: Light brn. 25"

A most lifelike figure, with soft detail giving this Mignon a youthful, angelic aura. Both bouquet and mandolin enhance composition. Foundry workmen's initials are incised on backside of piece.

### 702. MIGNON by Adrien-Etienne Gaudez
c1890. Fr. Pt: Brown. 12"

This is Gaudez's delightful interpretation of Mignon. At time of its introduction, Gaudez had already attained the honorary distinction of "Hors Concours" ("above competition").

### 705. MIGNON by Auguste Moreau
c1900. Fr. Pt: Dk. brn. 18"

Sitting on rock with mandolin in lap, Mignon is captured in a forlorn and pensive mood. Square slab of bronze forms second base. Hair and face are lifelike. Fingers and toes are worked to perfection.

**701**

**702**

705

708

**710**

**714**

718

719

708. SPRING by Etienne-Henri Dumaige
c1870. Fr. Pt: Chocolate. 17½"

Up-sweep of hairdo emphasizes contour of figure's lovely neckline. Position of head and facial expression similar to Fig. 705. Statue stands on fine, red marble base.

*Hudelet*

710. UN JOUEUR DE DES
by Henri-Paul Hudelet
1877. Fr. Pt: Gold enamel. 16"

Excellent composition of figure in Hudelet's study of young boy engrossed in dice game. Closeup view shows disintegrating enamel patina as well as fine line where arm is fitted perfectly into body.

714. JEUNE ET CHATTE
by Clement-Leopold Steiner
c1885. Fr. Pt: Dk. brn. 25"

Boy, with playful cat, was originally sculpted nude, but for popular bronze edition a scant covering was added. Figure stands on green and black marble base.

718. WINNER OF THE COCK FIGHT
by Jean-Alexandre-Joseph Falguiere
1864. Fr. Pt: Brown. 31"

Inspired by sculpture of "Mercury," Figure 719, Falguiere's work created much attention, and the Louvre, Paris, acquired it for its collection. Originally exhibited nude, Thiebaut Brothers Foundry clothed the figure and produced this popular edition under their seal.

Solid balance on small circular base was achieved by sculptor centering boy's body and head above the one leg. By casting toes and lower leg as part of base, and then anchoring section from beneath with eight screws (see inset photo), founder gave durability to piece. Hollow arms and legs are pinned to torso.

719. MERCURY by Jean de Bologne
1564. Ital. Pt: Black. 23½"

Famous sculpture of Bologne presents Mercury as patron god of medicine and healing, just one of the deity's many roles in mythology. Many editions of this work were produced over the centuries; individual quality, condition and completeness would be the criteria for determining value. Figure shown here, with all elements intact, was cast circa 1800.

720. PROUD FATHER by Antonio Pandiani
1889. Ital. Pt: Yellow. 15"

Well-to-do father, with head high, cigarette between lips, and cloak thrown fashionably over one shoulder, struts proudly down street with daughters. Lady in center appears to be shy and modest, but her sister, with flirtatious expression and posture, is much the contrary. Together, the three figures present a study in contrasts; individually, a study of character and personality.

Milanese foundry work, of which this is an example, was of unsurpassed quality. Because production was limited, and of a specialized nature, Italian founders never were able to truly compete with the giants of Europe.

# L.Domenech

723. MESSAGER DE PAIX
by Luis Domenech Y Vicente
1904. Fr. Pt: Black. 38"

The "messenger of peace," young and powerful, firmly holds shaft of spear and flowers in one hand while other hand, open, offers peace. Figure won Honorable Mention of Salon 1904. Although not apparent from this work, Vicente was noted for his stylized Art Nouveau pieces.

724. FORGERON DE LA PAIX by G.B. Germain
1904. Fr. Pt: Black. 38"

Smith at anvil is turning weapons of destruction into implements of peace. This fine work, cast in white metal, took second prize in "Peace" competition in Salon of 1904.

720

**724**

**723**

MESSAGER DE PAIX

732

733

734

735

736

737

738

739

# ARThUR-BOURGEOIS

**731. CHARMEUR DE SERPENTS**
by Baron Charles-Arthur Bourgeois
1863. Fr. Pt: Dk. brn. 22½"

Agile, muscular African dances in rhythm to tune
he plays on primitive fife as he charms asp coiled at
striking range. For grace, realism and composition,
this piece approaches perfection. Large, round
second base of marble gives figure added stability.
Bronze shown here is from original edition;
recasts have muted detail and thick, partially
fused fingers.

Bourgeois' works, all highly realistic, include bas-
reliefs, busts, reptiles, and mythological groups.

**732. RUN!** by Leblune
c1910. Ger. Pt: Grey
Ht: 3½"  Length: 8"

Whimsical miniature sculpted in technique that
simulates wood carving. Unadorned rectangular
base has bronze seal of register and guarantee.

**733. RAPE OF A SABINE WOMAN**
by Jean de Bologne
1580. Ital. Pt: Green. 20"

Sculpture, originally rendered in marble, has inspired numerous editions, as well as various versions
of the subject. Figure shown here, circa 1800, was
one modified to cover nudity of its three figures by
skillfully adding single length of draped cloth;
Statue rests on its original red marble base.

**734- SMALL ORNAMENTAL FIGURES**
**739.** c1900. Aus.

| | | |
|---|---|---|
| 734. | Pierrot and Drum | 5" |
| 735. | Zither Player | 3½" |
| 736. | Shopkeeper | 5½" |
| 737. | Tantrum | 5" |
| 738. | Negative | 6" |
| 739. | Pandora | 6½" |

742

744

750

751

747

749

742. BUTTERFLY by Auguste Moreau
1880. Fr. Pt: Yellow-brn. 30"

Young maiden, elbow resting upon ivy-draped pillar, appears totally absorbed in antics of butterfly perched on foliage in her hand. Bronze was edited by E. Godeau, Paris, foundry that cast majority of unmarked Moreau sculptures. Figure is supported on red marble base contoured to match base of sculpture.

In similar piece, "A Dangerous Find," Moreau uses same model but sculpts her nude, and instead of butterfly, she holds tiny Cupid. Exhibited in Salon of 1879, it was considered a tasteless and daring work of art, according to Victorian standards; hence, it was never cast.

744. THE RING by Jean-Louis Gregiore
c1880. Fr. Pt: Natural yellow. 20½"

Scene from opera "Faust" in which Faust offers ring to Marguerite. These figures also were produced as individual pieces, mounted on separate bases, and sold as a pair. Only modification from this edition was in figure of Faust, whose left hand is lowered to side as other hand offers a flower instead of ring. Cast by Sussi Brothers, Paris.

747- FAUST AND MARGEURITE
749. by Adrien-Etienne Gaudez
c1885. Fr. Pt: Brown. 17"

Costumes are much simpler on this pair as compared to Gregiore's Faust and Marguerite in Figure 744. Figures are not clothed in precise attire of period, nor are they depicted in specific scene from Gounod's opera, yet it was Gaudez's intention they represent the two characters. Sculpture was cast by Louchet, Paris, and sold through its undated, illustrated catalogue.

750- HE & SHE LAMPS by R. Bahnert
751. c1920. Ger. Pt: Dk. brn. 6"

Solid-cast night-table lamps have bronze, bowl-shaped shades. Small bulbs, now obsolete, emit dim light on interesting little figures.

752. DELIGHTED
c1910. Aus. Pt: Lt. brn. 4½"

Missing from piece is an object, probably a flower, which formed focal point of composition and reason for girl's delighted expression. Note hole below her toes, which is where object was originally attached.

753. EXUBERANCE
c1920. Aus. Pt: Multi-color paint. 6½"

Well done figure, with fine detail, captures mood of joy and gaiety. Bronze is solid-cast, in one piece, using complex mold.

754. HEXAGON VASE by Leon Kann
1906. Fr. Pt: Natural yellow. 5"

Art Nouveau-styled bowl, with inner removeable bronze cup, won prize of 1906 Salon. Cast in limited, numbered edition by Siot, Paris.

756. LA GASCOGNE by Lavergne
c1870. Fr. Pt: Brown. 14"

Graceful sculpture of lad as he runs alongside hoop directing it straight to the seashore (plaque), with skill and poise. Period costume adds to charm of piece.

757. BALANCING
c1920. Aus. Pt: Black. 8"

Lady performer, centerpiece for round marble ashtray, displays her form and skill. Figure, solid-cast in one piece, was produced in a complex mold.

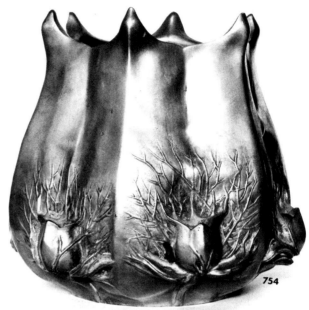

752

753

754

756

757

758

759

761

762

763

764

766

768

770

771

772

773

774

775

758-  SHEIK & HAREM GIRL by Louis Hottot
759.  c1875. Fr. Pt: Multi-color paint. 24" x 15"

Rare set of Hottot-signed bas-relief plaques, mounted in plain, heavy maplewood frames. Varying surface textures and types of paint present an interesting effect, while extensive detail adds to impression of realism, basic goal of both sculptor and founder.

761.  LEOPARD-KEEPER INK WELL
       c1900. Aus. Pt: Multi-color paint.
       Ht: 11"   Length: 19"

Fine African figure holds chains while walking pair of trained royal leopards. Two lidded ink-pots, set on polished black slate, complete bronze grouping.

762.  OWL
       c1910. Aus. Pt: Multi-color paint. 1½"

Solid-cast, chased, and hand-painted miniature could function as paperweight. Similar bronzes are now being produced, but casting and chasing are noticeably inferior. Original old pieces were rarely signed, but often are incised with the word "Austria."

763.  GOATHERD ASH TRAY
       c1910. Aus. Pt: Brown. 4"

Goat and figure are set on heavy, round, black marble ash tray. Goat, with mind of its own, appears to be at end of its rope.

764.  ELEPHANT LAMP
       c1920. Aus. Pt: Multi-color paint. 13"

Small bulb, hidden by palm leaves, emits soft indirect light, illuminating elephant. All parts of piece are bronze.

766.  STORK & FISH by Agathon Leonard
       c1885. Fr. Pt: Dk. brn. 13"

One contraction of bird's muscular neck, like cocking of a rifle, and fish will be swallowed and out of sight.

Leonard, sculptor who rendered this outstanding study, is noted for his skill in handling diverse subjects, from animals to Art Nouveau dancers (Loie Fuller).

# A.LEONARD

# C.Anfrie

768.  STANDARD BEARER by C. Anfrie
       c1890. Fr. Pt: Choc. brn. 24"

Heroic 65th Infantry Regiment is immortalized in this patriotic bronze. Base is equipped with swivel apparatus.

Anfrie is best known for sculptures of cherubs and elegant female figures.

770.  BEDTIME by Tuch
       c1920. Ger. Pt: Green. 9"

Dull satin patina, with dashes of color, gives woman's flesh realistic appearance.

771.  SHY by Franz Iffland
       c1910. Ger. Pt: Yellow. 6"

Sculptor captures "painfully shy" and embarrassed expression of modest young girl.

772.  NUDE & BIRD by Schwatenberg
       c1900. Ger. Pt: Green. 9"

Bird perched on lady's raised elbow forms focal point for composition of nude sculpture.

773-  FUNCTIONAL ART NOUVEAU FIGURES.
775.  Unsigned.
       1910-1920.
       773.   NYMPH Ink & Pen Holder   15"
       774.   BACCHANTE Table Lamp   16"
       775.   FAIRY Candlestick          12"

776

777

778

779

780

781

782

783

784

786

787

788

789

790

791

792

793

794

776. VOLTAIRE by Jean-Antoine Houdon
c1850. Fr. Pt: Lt. grn. 5"

Exceptionally fine miniature bust faithfully reduced, from Houdon's larger-than-life monument, and cast by Decauville.

777. DOWN HILL
c1910. Aus. Pt: Multi-color enamel. 1½"

Fine, sub-miniature action piece mounted on snow-white marble.

778. SATYR ON TURTLE
c1850. Fr. Pt: Gold. 7"

Candelabrum held under arms of baby satyr, whose hoofs are implanted on shell of slow-moving tortoise. Original marble base supports this interesting group.

779- BIRD BASKETS
780. c1920. Aus. Pt: Multi-color enamel. 5"

Beautiful and intricate detail in each element——bird, basket and flowers——of these very realistic bronze sculptures.

781. SOLDIER
c1870. Rus. Pt: Black. 3½"

Tiny full-length figure, exhibiting good detail for its size, is rendered in excellent proportion. For sake of comparison, length of musket is that of a toothpick.

782. PEAR INKWELL by Louis Kley
c1875. Fr. Pt: Choc. brn. 5"

Pear, on antique red beveled marble, opens on rear hinge. Pouting baby appears to be guarding ink.

783. NUDE BOY by Franz Barwig
c1890. Aus. Pt: Light green.
Ht: 3½"  Length: 9"

Pleasing figure done in typical Barwig style, with soft detail, yet bold, angular and modern.

784. CHORES by Raphael Hubert
c1920. Fr. Pt: Brown. 9½"

Solid bronze casting of peasant girl performing chores. Imperfections in patina are visible.

786. PECHEUSE by Adrien-Etienne Gaudez
c1895. Fr. Pt: Dk. brn. 18"

This attractive lady putting catch in her basket, may not be wearing fishing-attire of the day, but she certainly made a charming model for Gaudez's theme.

787- HUNTER & FARMER by Victor Novak
788. c1905. Ger. Pt: Yellow-grn. 6½"

Cherubian hunter and farmer are both rendered in somewhat modern stylized design that facilitates molding and casting.

789- SIT & PUSH BOOKENDS by Paul Silvestre
790. c1920. Fr. Pt: Dk. grn. 4"

Art Deco styled figures on bookends, bearing seal of Sussi Brothers Foundry, represent reduced version of male and female satyrs in "Miroir D'eau" fountains in Paris and Lucerne.

791- DUTCH PAIR
792. c1910. Aus. Pt: Brown. 4"

Matching small figures, such as this Dutch girl and boy, usually served as decorative pieces for desk or mantle. Note arms and legs are not fused as in figures 793 and 794.

793- NIGHT-LIGHTS
794. c1920. Aus. Pt: Grn. & brn. paint
Ht., figure only: 3"

Sculpting of figures with arms and legs fused to body permits use of simplest, and least expensive, molding and casting procedures.

795

797

799

# Schœnewerk

795. DAY DREAMS by Schoenewerk
     c1860. Fr. Pt: Dk. brn. 12"

Seated figure presents interesting composition of lovely lady deeply absorbed by her innermost thoughts. Magnificent detailing of folds in gown and styling of hairdo demonstrates Schoenewerk's artistic skill, as well as founder's high quality workmanship.

797. MOTHER & SON. Unsigned.
     c1850. Fr. Pt: Black. 11"

Exaggeration or over-emphasis of detail is sculptor's special style in this fine unsigned work. Piece is hollow cast, thin.

799. PHYRNE by Jean-Jacques Pradier
     c1840. Fr. Pt: Yellow-grn. 12"

Partially nude figure is sculpted in classic Grecian style and posture; note preciseness of folds in draped garment as it hangs down thigh to toes. Cast by Sussi Brothers Foundry, this work has appeared under various titles, among which were "Phyrne" (as acknowledged here), "Venus Sortant du Bain," and "La Nymphe au Bain."

# FOUNDERS
*Keyed to the Photographic Section*

A.B.
210  354

ANYZ
787  788

A.R.
381  615

BARBEDIENNE, F.
162  183  185  218  398
485  499  521  528  679

B.D.
723

BERGMAN
121  153  616  620  659
664  665  761

BERNEAUX
479  545

C.E.
770

C & L
168

COLLIN & Cie.
235  237  671  672

COTTIN, R.
214  692

DALE Co., C.B.
642

ETAT
693

FABRICATION FRANCAISE
294  339  400  403  442
536  774

FIELD Co., Marshall
225  229

FRIEDENAU, A. Noack
688

GLADENBECK & SOHN
136  148  150  152  314
417  512  697

GODEAU, E.
116  257  262  441

GOUPIL & Cie.
687  747  749

JULLIEN, E.
100  292  293

KUNST, K.K.
448  611

LOUCHET
411  608

L.U.
174

L.V.
555  637

MIROY Fres.
425  427

OPITZ, O.
690

PANDIANI, A.
720

PETERMANN, J.
373  374

PINEDO
554

POTET, L.
326

QUESNEL, E.
532

SANSON OF HAMBURG
401

ST. PETERSBURG
318

SIOT DECAUVILLE
186  193  234  379  566
582  754  776

SOCIETE DES BRONZES
269  274  299  301  323
366  372  635  636

SUSSE (SUSSI) Freres
251  432  452  560  569
573  744  789  799

THIEBAUT
656  718

TIFFANY & Co.
548  593  634

WIEST
192  458

ZERRITSCH, F.
460

# SCULPTORS
*Keyed to the Photographic Section*

AIZELIN Eugene-Antoine
573

ANFRIE C.
241 444 768

ANTONI
248

AURIRIEDRIA Victor
558

BAHNERT R.
750 751

BARBEDIENNE Ferdinand M.
182 184 185 218 485 521

BARRIAS Louis-Ernest
398 399

BARTLET E.
215

BARWIG Franz
783

BARYE Antoine-Louis
330

BECK
690

BERGMAN R. P.
616

BERGMAN
121 153 227 620 644 665 761

BESSERDIGI
556

BOFILL Antoine
168

BOLOGNE Jean de
719 733

BONHEUR Marie-Rosalie
333

BOSIO baron Francois-Joseph
382 383

BOURET Eutrope
393 468 601 609 640

BOURGEOIS baron Charles-Arthur
731

BREUER Peter
148

BROSE Carl
482

BRUTT Adolf-Karl-Johannes
105

BUICE
562

CALLOT Jacques
237

CARLIER Emile-Joseph-Nestor
464

CARRIER BELLEUSE Albert-Ernest
210 475 488 517

CARTIER Thomas-Francois
339

CAUSSE Cadet-Julien
586

CERIBELLI Cesar
629

CHARRON Alfred-Joseph
555

CHEMILLIER George de
607

CHERET Joseph-Gustave
188 192

CLODION Claude-Michel
345 360 361 489 495 612

COLLE Charles-Alphonse
172

CORDIER Charles-Henri-Joseph
581

COUDRAY Marie-Alexandre-Lucien
269 274

CULUCHE L.
409

CUMBERWORTH Charles
452

CURTS T.
342

DALE C. B. Co.
642

DEBUT Jean-Didier
535 542

DEBUT Marcel
178

DERNIERE
778

DOMENECH Y VICENTE Luis
723

DROUOT Edouard
414

190

DUBOIS Paul
156  166  528
DUBOY Paul
466
DUCHOISELLE
509
DUMAIGE Etienne-Henri
510  708
DURET Francisque-Joseph
532
DUTRION
311  457
EICHLER Theodor-Karl
541
EUSELE
522
FALGUIERE Jean-Alexandre-Joseph
718
FAURE de BROUSSE Vincent-Desire
201  354
FERRAND Ernest-Justin
307
FIELD Marshall
225
FIORUCCI M.
599
FOUQUET Emile-Francois
256  520
FREMIET Emmanuel
378  596
FRITZSCHE Marcus
651
GARNIER J.
401
GAUDEZ Adrien-Etienne
644  675  702  747  749  786
GAUTIER Gerald
463
GERMAIN G. B.
724
GIESSERET
448
GLADENBECK & SOHN
148  152  512  697
GODET Henri
357  637
GOLDSCHEIDER
171
GOTZ Johannes
417

GREGOIRE Jean-Louis
432  479  545  560  744
GRUNDMANN B.
149
GUILLEMIN Emile-Coriolan
550  552  686
GUILLOT Thomas-Anatole
292  293
GUIRANDE T. D.
138
GURSCHNER Gustave
592
HACKSTOCK K.
397
HAFNER
232
HEINGLE Anton
543
HERLINGER T.
244
HILLER C. J.
238
HOTTOT Louis
758  759
HOUDON Jean-Antoine
381  776
HUBERT Raphael
784
HUDELET Henri-Paul
710
HUZEL
421
IFFLAND Franz
181  182  771
JOUFFREY Francois
499
KAESBACH Rudolf
645
KANN Leon
754
KASSIN Joseph
240
KAUBA Carl
388  389  570  595
KESK
423
KINSBURGER Sylvain
434
KISS August-Karl-Eduard
314

# SCULPTORS

KLEY Louis
204 205 519 782

KNIGHT Charles-Robert
698

KORSCHANN Charles
688 688A

KRUSE Bruno-Friedrich-Emile
151 540

LAFON MOLLO
100

LANCERAY Ievgueni-Alexandro
318

LaPORTE Emile-Henri
524 604

LAOUST Andre-Louis-Adolphe
200

LARCHE Francois-Raoul
379 566

LAVERGNE Adolphe-Jean
410 756

LEBLUNE
732

LECORNET, Nicolas
251

LEGER Rene
109

LEMARQUIER Charles-Paul-Alfred
403 411

LEONARD Agathon
537 766

LeVASSEUR Henri-Louis
213

LEVEQUE Edmond-Louis
425 427

LILLO Ralph
309

LOISEAU ROUSSEAU Louis-Paul
459

LORMIER Edouard
387

MARIN Joseph-Charles
349 491

MARIOTON Eugene
622

MENE Pierre-Jules
327 328

MENGIN Paul-Eugene
648

MERCIE Marius-Jean-Antonin
679 687

MESTAIS
164

MIRO Rudolph
564

MIROY
425 427

MOIGNIEZ Jules
641

MONCEL Alphonse-Emmanuel
692

MORE
236 594

MOREAU Auguste
170 174 203 400 438 507 705

MOREAU Hippolyte-Francois
116 436 536 635 636 650 701

MOREAU Mathurin
113 257 262 366 441 509

MOREAU
224 447 650

MOULIN Hippolyte-Alexandre
502 505

NAM GREB
121 153 227 612 620 659 664

NEEB
512

NOVAK Victor
787 788

OGE Pierre-Marie-Francois
396

OPITZ O.
690

PALLEZ Lucien
242

PANDIANI Antonio-Agostino
720

PEYNOT Emile-Edmond
508 624

PICAULT Emile-Louis
214

PICCIOLE M.
408

PINEDO Emile
554

PIRON Eugene Desire
655

PLE Henri-Honore
569

POTET Loys Pierre
326

PRADIER Jean-Jacques
206 255 472 658 799
RALLENBERG Joseph F.
340
RANCOULET Ernest
358 359
RANIERE Aristide de
306
REITER Carl
202
RINGEL Maximilien-Victor
190
ROCHE Pierre
140
ROGER Francois
402 693
RUBIN Auguste
228
RUFF Andreas
154 470 557
SAALMANN E.
142
SALMSON Jean-Jules
646
SAINT MARCEAUX Charles-Rene
162
SAUTNER Franz-Adolph
320 338
SCHAFFERT
652 653
SCHOENEWERK Alexandre-Pierre
265 795
SCHWATENBERG
772
SCOTTE T.
634
SEIFERT Victor-Heinrich
150 152
SILVESTRE Paul
490 789 790
SIOT—DECAUVILLE
186 187 234
SOMME Theophile-Francois
310
SORNIN C. F.
608
STEINER Clement-Leopold
656 714
SUA Lenberti
282

SUAN FERVILLE
649
SUCHETET Auguste-Edme
235
SUTTON
176
THIERMANN
419
TIFFANY Louis-Comfort
548
TILGNER Victor-Oskar
460
TILLET Paul
249 431
TITZE A.
319 539
TOBLUEIGRTH
615
TUCH
770
UNGER Hella
611
VALLET Marius
582 584
VAN DER STRAETEN George
323 366 368 370 371 372 373 374
VAN DE VIN
590
VILLANIS Emmanuele
299 300 301 303 305 308 321 561
VINGTRIE Bayard
277
VITAL CORNU Charles
180
WAAGEN
289
WAGNER G.
286 445
WANTE E.
602
WERNEKINCK S.
136
WERNER Karl Joseph
448
WIEST
458
ZIELBAUER A.
577

*BRONZES, SCULPTORS & FOUNDERS*
*1800-1930, BOOK II, now in preparation,*
*will include signed bronzes by the sculptors*
*listed on this page.*

| | | | | |
|---|---|---|---|---|
| ADOLPHE | CHIPARUS, D. H. | GAFFEAD, G. | LeGULUCHE, J. | RHIND, M. |
| ALLOUARD | CICCHUTZZ | GARDEN, L. | LELIEVRE | RIVIERA, M. G. |
| ALONZO | CLARA, J. | GARDET, G. | LEPCKE, F. | ROCHARD, I. |
| ANGELO, E. | COLOMBO, R. | GARET, A. | LEVY | RODIN, A. |
| BACHMANN, M. | CONKLING, M. | GASQ, P. | LIPCHYTZ | ROSSI |
| BACQUE, D. | CONTI, P. | GECHTER, T. | LOREN, V. C. R. | ROUSSEAU |
| BAERER, H. | CONTINI | GAUGUIN, P. | LORENZ, L. | ROZET, F. |
| BAILLY, C. | CRADEK | GENNARELLI | MacMONNIES, F. | RUSSEL, C. |
| BARRE, A. | CROISY | GEROME, J. L. | MacNEIL, H. A. | SANSON, J. |
| BARTHOLEMY, L. | CROZATIER, C. | GIRARDET, B. | MADRASSI, L. | SAUVAGEAU, L. |
| BARYE, A. | CSADEK, T. | GIRARDON, F. | MARCUSE, R. | SCHIMMELPFENNIA |
| BAUER, M. | CURTS, T. | GIRON, E. | MASSON, C. | SCHLUTER, C. H. W. |
| BAVIL | DALLIN, C. E. | GORIANOV, A. | MERTH, G. B. | SCHUBEN, R. |
| BEACH, C. | DAMPT, J. A. | GORNIK, F. | MINNE, G. | SEIFERT, V. |
| BELLOC, J. B. | D'ASTE | GRANET, P. | MOIGNIEZ, J. | SEVIN |
| BEQUERELLE | DAUMIER, H. | GRATCHEFF | MOELLER, H. N. | SIENARD, E. |
| BERTHOUD | DeFIESOLE | GRATCHEV | MORAN, P. | SHRADY, H. M. |
| BIZAND, S. | DELABRIERE, P. | GURADZE, C. | MOREAU, L. | SOLDANI-BENZIM |
| BONCHE, J. | DELAPCHIER, L. | GUILLAUME, E. | MOREAU, V. | STELLA |
| BONEGIR, A. M. | DESCA | HAMANI | MULLER, H. | STRANTZ, A. |
| BONHEUR, I. | DETRIER | HOUDON, J. A. | NEMAR, E. | TABACCHI, O. |
| BONOME | DeWEVER, A. | HUMPHREYS, A. | NIEUWERKERKE | TERESZCZUK, P. |
| BORGHI, A. | DEUBY, M. | HUMPHRISS, C. H. | OMERTER, G. | TIOR, M. |
| BOURAINE, M. | DODGE, F. | HYATT, ANNA | PASCAL | TOURGUENEPP, P. |
| BOURGEOIS, M. L. | DRAPPIER, E. | INJALBERT, J. | PARIS, R. | TROUBETZKOY, P. |
| BOVEGZI, A. M. | DROUOT, E. | JACQUEMIN | PATENTE | TRUMPT |
| BRINES, J. F. | DUBUCAND, A. | JENSON, F. | PEYRE, C. R. | VALANTIN |
| BRUCHON, E. | DUCHOISELLE | KAAN | PEYROL, F. | VALTON, C. |
| CAIN, A. | DUMAGE, H. | KORBEL, MARIO | PHILIPPE, P. | VASSELOT, J. J. |
| CAMPAGNE, P. | EBERLE, A. | KOSSOWSKI, H. | POERTZEL | VIBERT, A. |
| CARDWELL, H. | FABERGE, K. | KOVALEZ | POWELL, G. | VICHI |
| CARO, F. L. | FERRARI, G. | KRACH | PREISS, F. | VIRIEUX, L. |
| CARPEAUX, B. | FLAMAND, G. | LAMBEAUX | PRIVAT, G. | WAAGEN |
| CHALON, L. | FLORA, F. | LAMBERT, N. M. | PROCTOR, P. | WAGNER, S. |
| CHAPU, H. M. A. | FRASER | LaMONACA | RASMUSSEN | WINDER, R. |
| CHARGEBAEDE | FRISHMUTH, H. | LAURENT, G. H. | RECIPON | WOERFFEL, C. F. |
| CHATEIGNON, J. | FROST, H. | LECOURTIER | REMINGTON, F. | WOLFF |
| CHECA | FUGERE, H. | LeFAGUAYS, P. | RENNER, F. | ZACK, B. |

# PART TWO
## General References

# Founders' Seals

Seals, generally found on medium and large sculptures, are round metal labels designating the founder's "guarantee." They came into common use during the last half of the 19th century, particularly in France.

A figure bearing a seal, whether it be bronze or white metal, invariably is a work of fine quality; however, its absence—same as that of a signature—does not imply lesser quality. Some of the finest pieces have no mark or identification of any kind; in fact, such is the situation with a great number of works produced.

Many smaller foundries that turned out beautiful pieces over the years used no mark or seal. On the other hand, there were others that inscribed their logo, name, or initials on each edition they cast. In instances where a sculptor was also a proprietor of a foundry—or where he directly employed the use of its facilities—he replaced the founder's mark with his own signature.

Seals are attached to or incised into the base of the figure, and they may be one of the following three types:

(1) SOLDER SEAL—metal tag soldered onto base. This type is found primarily on finer quality white-metal pieces.

(2) HAMMER SEAL—emblem hammered into the base by means, of a die, and has no metal added to it. This type of seal is quite small, and so, often goes undetected.

(3) MINTED SEAL—coin-like, fine quality bronze disc (similar in appearance to an American penny) pressed into a counter-sunk hole drilled halfway into the base.

Phrases or words commonly found appearing on seals are: Made by; Made of; Registered, trademarked, certified, guaranteed, copyrighted; Sculpted by; Method of manufacture; Method of fabrication; Special award won (giving place and year).

Words often used in association with producers of sculptures are: bronzier, editor, fabricator, founder ciseleur, chiseller, Freres, Fres, Succr, company, and manufacturer.

**196**

1

2

3

4

5

6

7

8

*SEALS are keyed to works pictured in the Photographic Section.*

1. **BRONZE GARANTI AU TITRE, PARIS**
   376  554

2. **BRONZE GARANTI AU TITRE, FRANCE**
   269

3. **F. P. SANSON SUCCR. NEUERWALL 4, HAMBURG**
   401

4. **VRAIS BRONCE DEPOSE K.**
   732

5. **ANDRE LAOUST NE A DOUAI 1843**
   200

6. **REDUCTION MECANIQUE, A. COLLAS BREVETE**
   162  499  528  679

7. **REDUCTION MECANIQUE, ACHILLE COLLAS, IVEY 1863**
   608

8. **SOCIETE DES BRONZES DE PARIS**
   274  301  323  366  368  371  372  635  636

9

10

11

12

13

14

15

16

*SEALS are keyed to works pictured in the Photographic Section.*

9.  THIEBAUT FRERES FONDEURS, PARIS
    718

10. BRONZES UNIS 1878
    648

11. LOUCHET CISELEUR, PARIS
    411

12. SUSSE FRERES EDITEURS, DE PARIS
    452   799   789   790

13. SOCIETE DES BRONZES, M. H.   1886
    370

14. EXPOSITION DE 1900 MEDAILLE D'OR M. D., PARIS
    170

15. EXPOSITION M. D. Mlle D'OR H. V., PARIS 1900
    326

16. MEDALLE D'OR M. D., PARIS
    299

17

18

19

20

21

22

23

24

17.  A.B., PARIS
     354

18.  VRAI BRONZE B. D. PARIS
     723

19.  R. COTTIN BRONZES, PARIS
     692

20.  FABRICATION FRANCAISE, MADE IN FRANCE, PARIS
     294  295  339  400  403  442

21.  BRONZE GARANTI AU TITRE DEPOSEE C&L
     168

22.  BRONZE GARANTI AU TITRE DEPOSEE L. V.
     555  637

23.  BRONZES PINEDO, Boule du temple 40 PARIS
     554

24.  SIOT DECAUVILLE FONDEUR, PARIS
     379  566  582  754

# Identifying Characteristics
# of Bronzes and White Metals

### Bronze vs. white metal

Works of art, in vast numbers, have been cast commercially in both bronze and white metal since mid-19th century. Many of the mold-making, finishing and patinization techniques for bronze and white metal are the same, so it was not unusual to find foundries producing pieces in both metals. Fabricators of the less expensive white metal would advertise their works as "simulating in every detail" and being "being able to pass" for costly bronzes.

Most beginning collectors, and some dealers as well, cannot readily, nor with certainty, distinguish one metal from another. In making superficial judgments, they will employ such unreliable criteria as weight, sound, size, signature, patina, subject, base, or price. And many will make purchasing decisions based on misconceptions and mislabeled merchandise.

Compounding the difficulties of identification of metals have been the all too common use of vague and misleading words, such as "bronzed, bronze metal, French bronze," etc. Anyone sincerely desiring to avoid misunderstanding should not arbitrarily use the word "bronze" when referring to a piece of sculpture, unless the figure is actually made of bronze.

### Comparative values

Many people are inclined to call white-metal pieces "fakes," "copies" or "imitations." Perhaps such references may have been appropriate when they were first produced, but today such terms no longer apply. A goodly number of white-metal pieces are extremely desirable and have values relative to their bronze counterparts; however, there is no specific formula as to what this relationship might be.

**200**

Some bronze collectors will invest in white-metal pieces when they find one that may be purchased at a price ratio of 1/4 to 1/5 that of similar quality bronzes. Knowledgeable interior decorators, on the other hand, when determined upon acquiring a particular piece for a particular setting will often pay for a white-metal figure up to ½ the price of a similar bronze, even if intending to refinish it to achieve a desired effect.

Whether it be bronze or white-metal composition, good sculptures will always find a ready market of buyers when priced "right." These metal figures are among the most difficult of antiques to be reproduced in a manner capable of passing as "old."

### What is bronze?

The word "bronze," if defined by its metallic composition alone, would not be a precise one, as it differs by historical period, country and use. 90% copper plus 10% tin, for example, is an alloy of bronze, but so is 90% copper + 7% tin + 3% zinc. When tin is omitted, the alloy becomes brass—copper + zinc.

Copper, the main ingredient of both brass and bronze, readily combines with zinc, lead, aluminum, nickel, tin or silver. In works of art, any alloy rich in copper may properly be considered bronze when given a patina.

In the past, it was the practice of founders to smelt whatever metals were available to them at the time. The quality of the finished bronze object, therefore, depended more on the foundry crafts—smelting, molding, chasing, patining—than on the exact metallic content.

For all practical purposes, the collector should consider yellow to tan the color of bronze metal.

### What is white metal?

Any alloy of zinc, lead, tin or other silver-colored metals, mixed in the "pot," is known as "white metal"—a definition even less precise than "bronze." Alloys of white metal are innumerable; on a quality scale they may range from "junk" to "fine."

The color of white metal is silver to silver-blue. It will never have any trace of yellow in its appearance, as copper is not one of its alloys. The basic reason for this is that copper's melting point is $1083°C$, while zinc, the main component of white metal, has a melting point of $420°C$ and a boiling point of $906°C$; obviously, the two metals will not combine properly into a castable alloy.

White metal, by simplest of terms for identification purposes, may be said to be a silver-colored metal.

### Improper methods for identifying metals

• BY COLOR. When a patina is applied to the surface of a figure, color no longer is a reliable method for identifying its metallic composition.

• BY WEIGHT. When cast to the same thickness, bronze and white metal will weigh approximately the same. Therefore, weight cannot be considered a positive method of identification.

• BY SOUND. When tapped or clicked with the fingers or a hard object, both bronze and white metal will resound with tones ranging from a high-pitched ring to a dull thud. The sound you get will be determined by the object you use in tapping the metal, thickness of the part tapped, and the shape, size and type of assembly of the complete piece. Tapping, in fact, is perhaps the poorest method for identifying metallic content.

• BY SIZE AND SUBJECT. Gigantic works, as well as miniatures, were cast in both bronze and white metal, irregardless of subject; therefore, size or subject of a figure will offer no clue to metallic content.

### Identification by visual inspection

• TOOL MARKS. Bronze sculptures will exhibit filing-marks (chasing) left by workmen's tools in cleaning of casts and improving figure detail. On some larger and better quality pieces, knurling of skin surfaces will be visible. White-metal works, on the other hand, by coming out of the mold in a more highly finished condition, will show fewer signs of hand filing.

• SECTIONING. Arms, legs and other appendages of bronze figures were sectioned together in a radial manner, with bracelets, sleeves, necklaces and belts often being used to conceal joints. Small drill holes, where pins have been forced in and ground off, are visible under a bronze's acid patina—and to a lesser degree under a paint finish.

• DETERIORATION. Bronzes do not pit nor rust; neither will they deteriorate beyond the tarnishing stage when they are exhibited only indoors. Constant outdoor exposure will result in a blue, green, or white powdery surface crust. White-metal figures when kept in a damp place may pit and corrode under their patina of paint.

• HOLES. Bronzes, generally, will not have air holes, as they are usually cast in sections. White-metal pieces, however, often cast as one complete form in a complicated mold, required air vents. Common to white-metal figures are irregular-shaped holes, resulting when metal fails to cover the entire mold; such holes are rare in bronzes, as each section was carefully inspected for such flaws.

- BASE. Fine, original marble bases were usually confined to quality bronzes. Bases used for white-metal figures often were made of inexpensive dyed marble, marble veneer over plaster, or wood painted to simulate marble.
- PATINA. Only bronze figures were given acid patinas; white-metal pieces were either painted or plated.
- DAMAGE. If dropped, bumped or lifted by appendages, bronzes will tend to loosen or detach at the joints; whereas white-metal figures, being of one-piece construction, generally will break or crack.

## Copper-plated figures

Some of the best bronze replicas are electrically plated pieces, employing a thin sheet of copper over plaster, porcelain or bisque figures, and they will have acid patinas. These pieces often are of good quality, and of considerable value in their own right; but, they are not bronze—and should be identified accordingly.

Copper-plated works may be detected in three ways:
(1) by lightly scraping the surface—in an inconspicuous spot, of course—to reveal the reddish color of copper;
(2) by gently tapping the piece to reveal areas in which the copper overlay has separated from the inner core; where this is the case, you'll hear a faint tinny sound; and
(3) by forcing a small nail deep into the underside, piercing the shell, to expose a white-colored, solid center core.

As plated figures are easily damaged, extra care should be exercised when lifting or moving them.

## Iron figures

Especially interesting are iron figures, which occasionally appear on the market. They are cast figures, of Russian and Western European origin, produced in the same fashion as bronzes. Since they were difficult to cast, they are quite rare. Their value approximates that of bronze works of equivalent quality.

## Alloy metal figures

Lastly, there is a whole area of fine metal figures which, on the quality scale, rightfully belongs somewhere between bronzes and white metals. These pieces are composed of a fine alloy of white metals, expertly cast and carefully finished. In good condition, such works may well have more value than many average bronzes. An astute collector should not pass up these fine metal figures when available at a fair price.

### Geiss' Zinc Castings (White Metal)

*The problem of positive and accurate identification is as old as the existence of white metal figures themselves—that is, from the time mass-produced "zinc" statuary first appeared on the market.*

*Best known of the early casters was Geiss of Berlin. Using technology developed by Belgian and German scientists, he was able to isolate pure zinc from ore. He first exhibited his "zincs," some of mammoth proportions, in the American Crystal Palace at the Great Exhibition in London, 1853.*

*The "Art Journal," in 1851, had this to say of Geiss and his works, "Zinc has been hitherto very little used in England; in Prussia, however, it has been resorted to, more or less, in nearly every structure of modern erection. M. Geiss has devoted his attention chiefly to the production of statues in zinc; the purity of the casts, the perfection of the chiselling, and durability of the material combine to recommend it, while the cost of zinc thus adopted, is about one-eighth of the cost of bronze".*

EDUCATION Unsigned
c1890 Fr. 24"

Decorative zinc figures and clock case of this type were very popular during the Victorian period. Their cost was several times less than similar mantle clocks cast in bronze.

# What Is Meant by Signed, Listed, Dated and Numbered

## I. SIGNED BRONZES

A signed bronze is one that contains a name or signature. It may appear on a title plaque that is attached to the base of the figure or to the marble base. In many instances, it is incised somewhere on the base of the piece itself. In either case, it would be referred to as a "signed" piece. Signed by whom?

• IN THE MOLD. If an original plaster or clay sculpture was signed by the sculptor, his signature would appear on all pieces in that edition. Often it would be deepened and refined by the foundryman as he routinely worked-up details in the mold or casting.

• INCISED. Many times an incisor, a foundry specialist, would tool a signature into the finished bronze. It would be executed in his own style or in one prescribed by the sculptor. Although skilled in his craft, the incisor was not always a literate individual—a fact which accounts for the frequent misspellings and irregularly formed letters found in signatures.

### Unsigned pieces

Many bronzes are not signed or marked in any way. Although collectors find this frustrating, some unmarked works may be quite valuable—and sometimes for the very reason that they are *not* signed.

205

• MINIATURES. Miniatures and small figures usually were unsigned, for the simple reason there was no suitable area in which to place the signature. Also, in the era when small-size figures were being produced, they were regarded as decorative items rather than works of art, and as such, a signature was of little value or importance.

On the bottom of many small pieces, the word "Austria" can be found die-incised in small letters. In fact, most of the small, solid bronze figurines (signed or unsigned) from the early 1900's were of Austrian origin. (Austria at that time included portions of what are now Poland, Czechoslovakia, Yugoslavia, Rumania and Italy.)

Many of these miniature figurines were done by in-house artists working at the foundry where they were cast. As employees, rather than independent artists, they tended to remain anonymous; a few notable exceptions, though, were Kauba, Nam Greb, Rubin, Tuch, Sautner, Tereszczuk, Seifert, Titze and Ruff. The works of these men were often signed but little noticed until the last decade.

• OLDER PIECES. Earlier sculptures are less apt to be signed. Signatures gradually came into vogue during the 19th century, along with literacy amongst the emerging middle class.

The first works of many sculptors were unsigned. But, as the man's works gained in popularity and his name became known, his signature became saleable and would appear on his later pieces. *Newer* sculptures, therefore, are more likely to carry a signature. Moreover, it is not unusual to find a sculptor's signature appearing on a reissue or recast of a popular work, although the original edition may not have had one.

Sometimes forged signatures are found on bronzes. They are added to enhance saleability of the piece to naive collectors who buy "names" and not esthetic qualities.

• MISCELLANEOUS REASONS for unsigned pieces:

(1) Lost bases or plaques. Lower bases and swivels on sculptures—where signature plaques were often affixed—were lost or left behind when being exported to the United States. A marble base may account for 50% of a figure's weight but only 10% of its sales value; and, since shipping charges were based on weight, it isn't surprising that many beautiful bases—along with their identification plaques—were left at the dock.

(2) Anonymous sculptors. While waiting to gain national commissions and exhibiting in salons, many talented—and now famous—sculptors executed frivolous or erotic works for foundries. They were reluctant to have their name appear on such pieces.

206

(3) Anonymous founders. Founders, too, often wanted to keep their identity a secret for various reasons. Sometimes it was to escape government regulations, inspection, or taxes; other times it was simply to be disassociated with erotic and pornographic works or with forgeries.

(4) Contracts. Contracts with sculptors would sometimes limit the number of signed pieces in a specific edition. Pieces that were cast thereafter—probably just as fine as the preceding quantity—bore no signature. Other contracts specified the length of time a foundry could place a signature on a figure; for example, two years could be the set time limit, and thereafter, it would be unsigned.

(5) Omission. Lack of time or simply a founder's oversight often resulted in unsigned works.

(6) Pairs. Occasionally, only one figure of a pair would be signed; so, when the two became separated, as they often did, one piece obviously lost its identification. Strangely, or by design, the male figure generally is the one carrying the signature.

(7) Reduced size figures. In some editions, only the larger size bears the signature; it was eliminated from the reduced version of the same work.

(8) Lesser quality line. Rejects or a cheaper production of a figure by a foundry often were left unsigned. Peddlers and young boys selling these statues were illustrated in many contemporary drawings.

## II. LISTED BRONZES

Listed by whom and where? In general, the term "listed" means that a particular sculptor's name appears alphabetically in a dictionary or encyclopedia, with reference to: place and date of birth and death, teachers and educational background, prizes or awards won, etc. French reference sources, naturally, favor French artists, listing more of them and in greater detail. German books, in the same manner, tend to give greater emphasis and space to German and Austrian sculptors.

It isn't unusual to find that some sculptors with minimal writeups—or none at all—are regarded as among the world's finest craftsmen. A case in point is C. Kauba, whose bronzes are perhaps the most coveted, versatile, and numerous. He is "unlisted." The large sums his pieces bring at auctions and private sales are an indication that his non-listed status carries no stigma with sophisticated bronze investors and collectors.

Nam Greb ("Bergman" spelled backwards) is another "unlisted" sculptor. His works, too, are numerous, fine, and highly prized, although he was not as versatile as Kauba.

Then there's F. Barbedienne, France's most prolific founder, who produced thousands of editions over more than half a century. Also he was a master sculptor of inkwells, candlesticks, urns, etc. Barbedienne is "unlisted."

E. Villanis, whose works were (and are) extremely popular, has only a minimal listing in a reference volume published in the very city where he worked for 25 years, sculpting hundreds of pieces.

Well-represented in listings are sculptors who won national and private commissions. Their monumental-size works which appear in parks, cemeteries and public lobbies, were not cast in smaller sizes; consequently, they are of little interest to collectors. Works of sculptors who did little exhibiting, but turned out statues in a more popular size and subject, were bought and cast for mass production by profit-motivated foundries. Bronze editions of such works are what's being collected today; but the sculptors who rendered them have shorter write-ups in reference books than the long-forgotten exhibitors.

## III. DATED BRONZES

Establishing the exact date of a casting is almost an impossibility. The date that oftentimes appears on a piece does not represent that of the cast. It usually identifies the year the original work was executed and/or exhibited by the sculptor.

### How can one estimate age?

Methods of casting have changed little over the period covered in this book. To determine the age of a bronze, a combination of features must be considered, such as signature, seal, founder, subject, style, patina, size, etc.

The signature, in particular, may be of some help in pin-pointing age as it establishes that the piece is no older than its sculptor; and, in all probability, it was not cast before he was 25 years of age. A signature, therefore, will narrow down the earliest date of origin, but can give no information as to how new it is. Many works of the last century are still being cast and recast.

### Old vs. new

There are new sculptures of living artists being cast today, in bronze, pewter and white metals. Some pieces are very well done and will certainly stand the test of time. These new figures, however, look nothing like the works of old, or even those of the 30's—and they are not meant to.

208

Fakes in the field of bronze-collecting are rare; to produce a passable one requires considerable expertise, time, facilities and materials.

## IV. NUMBERED PIECES

A number stamped on the base of a figure tells nothing. It was sometimes used for internal record-keeping or identification.

Numbers, when employed by a foundry, often did not follow any strict numbering system; more than one piece has been found to have the same number. Nor were numbers necessarily applied in consecutive order. First or tenth, however, is immaterial; molds did not deteriorate readily, and foundrymen were able to hold quality amazingly constant throughout an entire edition.

### Rarity

How rare is any particular bronze? As old foundry records are not available, and a number on a figure offers no clue, we shall never know how many pieces were produced in an edition.

Over the years, works have been widely dispersed; many have been destroyed, broken and melted down, all of which attribute to their rarity. In all probability, a few bronzes from each casting are still in existence. By chance, duplicate figures will surface in one area; yet that same work may never appear in an entire country.

All bronzes and white metals that are old may be regarded as "rare."

LADY Unsigned
c1925 France 6"

Highly stylized, yet lifelike, this
Art Deco piece exhibits fine
workmanship and has a base of white,
black and green marble. Patina is
painted in several shades of green—
a popular color during the 1920's
for metal sculptures.

# Characteristics and Identification of Patinas

A patina is the finish or fine covering applied to a metal object. Bronze sculptures usually have either an acid or paint patina. To determine whether a patina is acid or paint, scrape a small spot, in an inconspicuous area, on the backside of the figure. If fine particles appear to be separating, and they are not the same color as the exposed metal, the patina is paint. However, if no residue is evident upon scraping—only particles of metal—the patina is acid.

### Acid patina

To attain an acid patina, the surface of the figure is heated with a blowtorch and then brushed with various acids. The purpose of the heating process is to open the metal's pores and make them more receptive to the acids. Acids also may be applied to cold metal surfaces; this procedure, however, is used mainly on large figures which are to be situated outdoors.

Actually four basic steps are involved in putting an acid finish on a bronze: (1) Heating the surface with a torch; (2) applying the acid with a brush; (3) washing the figure in cold water at intervals, in order to keep the coating thin; and (4) repeating the cycle until the desired effect is achieved.

An acid patina improves in appearance with age. Its color deepens and the translucency, light reflections and luster of the various metals in the bronze tend to enhance its appeal.

An acid patina never flakes nor peels, because the finish is in the metal and formed, in part, through chemical fusion. Being of a porous nature, however, it spots and stains readily and permanently. Frequently an acid finish is mistaken for surface tarnish and is inadvertently removed in the process of cleaning or polishing.

## Paint patina

The first coating of a paint patina is generally a primer, which enters the pores of the metal only partially, and therefore, becomes susceptible to chipping and peeling, particularly from age and certain environmental conditions. A paint patina, however, generally is not affected by water or foreign substances; should a stain or spot occur, it can be readily removed with a cleaning agent.

Brushing, spraying, dipping, or a combination of these processes are the methods by which a bronze acquires a paint patina. A paint patina may be only one color, painted in a manner to simulate an acid finish, or it may be multi-color, in keeping with the varied tastes, specialties and fads of the period.

## Other considerations

Which of the two patinas adds more value to a bronze, acid or paint? The answer is neither. The condition of the patina is the determining factor when considering value.

Neither can the patina be considered when attempting to ascertain age of a figure. Two master French patinuers, Pere and Lean Limet, for example, working up until World War II, used the same methods and materials of the French foundries of 1850-1900—and achieved identical results. Also, acid and paint for patinas were used concurrently over the centuries, with German and Austrian founders favoring paint and the French, to a large extent, exhibiting preference for the more costly and difficult acid patinas.

In observing bronzes and their patinas, one notes that no two are exactly alike. Differences, however slight in some instances, may be attributed to: (1) Variation in acid formula used and strength or percentage of the chemicals contained therein; (2) number of applications or coatings; (3) degree of heat applied; (4) metallic content; (5) type of surface texture; and (6) age. And if we add to this list such factors as lighting and individual perception, we have a broad range of possible explanations.

## Bronze patining

For the technical-minded collector, here are six formulas for attaining desirable effects or finishes on most bronzes—those having an alloy content of 90% copper, 7% tin and 3% zinc.

| | | | |
|---|---|---|---|
| *Yellowish green:* | Color is obtained by using a solution of | | |
| | Ammonium chloride | 3½ | lbs. |
| | Copper acetate | 2 | lbs. |
| | Water | 1 | gal. |
| *Apple green:* | Sodium chloride | 20 | oz. |
| | Ammonia | 16 | fluid oz. |
| | Ammonium chloride | 20 | oz. |
| | Vinegar | 1 | gal. |
| *Bluish green:* | Sodium thiosulphate | 1 | oz. |
| | Nitrate of iron | 8 | oz. |
| | Water | 1 | gal. |
| *Antique green:* | Copper sulphate | 12 | oz. |
| | Ammonium chloride | 2 | oz. |
| | Water | 1 | gal. |
| | Rinse in cold, then hot water. | | |
| *Shades of brown:* | Potassium sulphide | 2 | oz. |
| | Barium sulphide | 4 | oz. |
| | Ammonia | 8 | fluid oz. |
| | Water | 3 to 5 | gals. |
| *Antique effect:* | Wash the bronze with nitrate of copper. Let it dry. Add a thick coating of nitrate of copper. Stipple with sal ammoniac and pulverized modeling clay. Add a little powdered chalk. Atomize entire surface with milk. Let this dry, and colors will be set. | | |

**TIGER ATTACKING ELEPHANT**
China c1900 7"

Bronzes of this type featured deeply etched surfaces and rich, red patinas. The methods and formulas used by the Orientals, to achieve these effects, are not known.

# Care, Cleaning and Polishing of Bronzes

**Caring for a bronze**

Giving a bronze proper care is basically a matter of knowing what *not* to do to it. Observing the following seven major "don'ts" can keep you from damaging the patina or finish of valued pieces in your possession.

(1) Don't apply *anything* to the surface of a bronze without first trying it on some obscure spot on the *back* side of the piece.

(2) Don't use soap or water for cleaning, as either can cause staining.

(3) Don't place any sharp or pointed object—whether it be glass, wood, or metal—near a bronze. This precaution will avoid any chance of accidentally chipping or scratching the finish.

(4) Don't use metal objects or wire brushes and don't apply abrasives, such as cleansers; these materials will scratch the finish.

Oftentimes what appears to be dirt actually may be the original finish. Crevices and deep corners, for example, frequently were finished in a darker patina (and should be left as originally applied).

Also, a bronze may have patches of lighter toned areas, which can lead one to believe an overall cleaning is needed. The figure simply may have had some of its natural oxidation rubbed off in these areas by hand contact during lifting or moving.

(5) Don't keep a paint-finished bronze near a radiator or heating unit. Extreme dry air will cause rapid deterioration and chipping.

(6) Don't try to match paint and touch up chipped spots on painted patinas. Don't try to match the color of acid patinas.

Although you may succeed in matching color, the luster or gloss may not be the same as that of the original. It is far better to leave the natural imperfections on a finish than risk having the saleability and value of a figure diminished by retouching.

(7) Don't use spray-can materials containing varnish or lacquer to coat the surface of a bronze, as the chemicals or thinning agents could either run or dissolve the finish.

Another objection to lacquers or sealing coats is their highly reflective gloss, which is detracting and tends to lessen the inherent aesthetic qualities of bronze sculptures.

### Cleaning a bronze

Before cleaning the surface of a bronze figure, it would be wise to determine what kind of finish or patina you'll be working on. Is it a painted or varnished patina, or is it an acid patina? Once you know this important consideration, you are ready to proceed.

If you are cleaning a painted patina, first remove surface dust and dirt by wiping the figure thoroughly with a damp cloth. If dirt still appears to be adhering, go over it again with a sponge, using one rubbed with a mild soap and squeezed almost dry.

If you are cleaning an acid patina, which has a more durable finish, you may tackle the surface grime more aggressively. Paint flecks, drippings, or any foreign matter may be removed by applying pressure with a blunt wood tool or object. An ice cream bar stick, for example, would do for this purpose as its edge is hard enough to dislodge adherences, yet soft enough not to scratch the finish. To dislodge imbedded material from deep crevices—such as eyes, ears, folds in garments, etc.—try using a toothpick; although this procedure may be slow and tedious, there is none better for accomplishing this task.

The last step in cleaning an acid patina requires swabbing of its surface—first with a slightly damp sponge containing a mild soap and then with a soapless sponge.

### Polishing a bronze

The final operation in attaining a bright clean look from a dull lifeless finish is polishing. Any of the following materials may be used in polishing of a bronze figure; all are safe to apply on any type of finish:

• SILICONE GUN-POLISHING RAG. To bring out natural-looking highlights, rub the treated cloth vigorously over the figure. As the surface of the piece picks up silicone, the finish becomes more lustrous with each stroke.

• TRANSPARENT LEATHER PRESERVATIVE. Apply the preservative to a damp cloth and wipe it over the bronze's surface. Next, rub the finish briskly with a soft dry rag. The more you continue to rub, the higher the luster.

• LIGHTWEIGHT LOCK OR WATCH OIL. Apply the oil with a long-bristled paint brush, covering its metal collar with tape to eliminate chance of scratching the finish. Dab the oil-laden brush over the entire figure, making sure the long bristles reach into all crevices. The piece should then be allowed to set, so that excess oil may drip off; after a few minutes, wipe the surface gently with a soft cloth, leaving the figure with a pleasing moist look.

To keep your bronze looking its best, repeat the polishing procedure once or twice a year. Although an oil polish will pick up dust more readily, and will not last as long as the gun-rag polish or leather preservative, it'll require relatively less time to apply.

PIERROT & PIERRETTE Unsigned
c1930 American 5½"

This small pair of metal pieces. set on marble, were originally lamp bases.
Any figures that have bone, ivory, Ivorene or marble parts require extra caution when cleaned and polished. Use of chemicals can permanently stain these porous materials. Polishing can easily loosen attached parts.

# Applying
# Your Own Patina

When the original patina on your bronze or white metal figure is in very poor condition, or if it has been removed for one reason or another, you may consider refinishing it. By following the procedure outlined here, you should be able to apply a patina that will pass for original to all but an expert.

### Materials
- Spray-can of red oxide enamel primer. This may be purchased at any paint supply store.
- Spray-can of dull-finish enamel in yellow, tan, gold or nutmeg. A semi-gloss enamel will not do; it *must* be a dull (matte) finish.
- Small tube of brown oil paint.

(Burnt Sienna oil paint applied over a nutmeg color of dull enamel will produce a beautiful patina in chocolate brown.)

### Steps in preparation and application
(1) Clean figure thoroughly. Use a Soilax solution; apply several times, and rinse carefully after each application.
(2) Open metal's pores. Use a mild ammonia solution; apply several times, rinsing thoroughly after each application.
(3) Let figure dry thoroughly. It should set overnight; even a drop of moisture can ruin the spray finish.
(4) Spray entire piece with a primer coat, following directions stated on container. Be sure coating reaches all crevices, which may mean putting figure on its side or turning it upside down. A thin coat is all that is needed. It is important that you do not let the primer run, as that is a dead giveaway of an amateur finishing job.

216

(5) Use the dull-finish enamel and repeat procedure no. 4. Allow figure to set for *several* days before beginning final application—regardless of what the directions tell you to the contrary!

(6) Squeeze oil paint onto a towel-like material and rub into figure. Apply oil liberally, and be sure to get into all corners and crevices. (For this step, it is suggested that old clothing be worn; also be aware of the fact you may end up with stained hands.)

(7) Wipe off excess oil paint immediately, using a soft terrycloth rag.

(8) With another rag, buff the figure's surface until gloss shows through on high areas. The effect will be an age-worn look, as tip of nose and other smooth high-spots reveal the underpaint.

Patience is the keyword when applying a patina to one of your statues. No step along the way should be rushed; an entire job may be ruined at any one point.

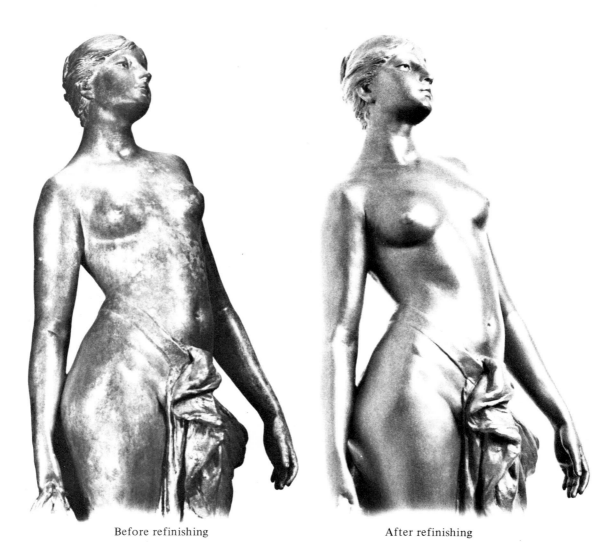

Before refinishing      After refinishing

# How to Photograph Bronzes

If you would like to photograph your collection of bronzes—whether it be for purposes of insurance appraisal, cataloguing, or personal enjoyment—here is a relatively simple but effective technique that requires very little equipment. It was the method used in photographing the statues appearing in this book. By following the instructions and diagram, you should be able to get excellent pictures of your bronzes—each figure outlined against a white background and minus distracting shadows.

### Required materials

- Camera with time-exposure setting, flexible shutter-release cable, and lens that stops down to increase depth of field and has standard sun-shade.
- Fine grain film, to accommodate 35mm. black-and-white enlargements. Kodak Plus X film is best for 5 x 7" prints; Panatomic X, for 8 x 10's.
- Sturdy tripod.
- Backdrop. Roll of coarse, white, dull-finish paper will do.
- Table or pedestal.
- Reflecting screen with stand, such as used for home-movie viewing.
- Diffusing screen. One may be inexpensively constructed from spun-glass (available at most camera shops) or from a sheet of single-weight white tissue paper; it is then stapled to a yardstick and suspended from a coat-rack (or similar mobile contrivance). It should be noted, though, that paper will ignite if placed too close to a hot bulb; a screen of such construction, therefore, can be a fire hazard.
- One 500W photo floodbulb, with 8-10" safety reflector.

### Setting up the equipment

• BACKDROP. Attach roll of paper to wall or ceiling trim, well above statue and about 2 ft. behind it; let it curve gently under the figure and drop off the front of pedestal. Set camera on tripod and center subject in viewfinder. Move or rotate bronze so that it appears at its most interesting angles.

• LIGHTING. Mount 500W floodbulb and reflector slightly above subject, positioning it 2 ft. right or left of camera and approximately 6 ft. from figure. Place diffusing screen halfway between light and subject; in this manner only filtered or diffused light reaches the statue, producing soft highlights and partially lighted shadow areas.

• REFLECTING SCREEN. To redirect light from floodbulb back onto far side of piece, position reflecting screen on opposite side of light source and slightly in front of subject. In contrast to the highlights and shadow patterns resulting from semi-direct or diffused light, the reflected light will be flat and even.

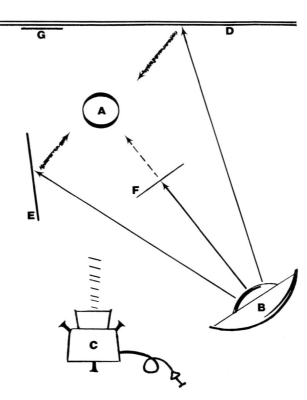

KEY

A. Art object
B. Light source
C. Camera
D. Backdrop
E. Reflecting screen
F. Diffusing screen
G. Shadow

------  Direct light
------  Diffused light
------  Reflected light
//////  Lens divergence

To make sure no conflicting reflections appear, block out light from windows and doorways. Your workroom lights, of course, should be turned out before starting the actual photographing operation.

With diffused light directed onto the subject from one side and reflected light from the other, the resulting photographs will convey a feeling of realism, an illusion of three dimension.

Before exposing the film, it would be wise to experiment with the equipment. Try moving the light, the screens, the subject, and then checking each change in the viewfinder. If the figure appears to be casting a shadow on the backdrop, it may be remedied by raising the light, moving the light more to the side, or sliding the statue forward to allow greater distance between it and the backdrop.

To reduce glare and soften lighting, move the diffusing screen closer to the subject. To increase highlights, move the screen closer to the light.

### Settings and exposures

To photograph bronze figures, use black-and-white film. The added expense of color is of doubtful value when recording tones of black or brown. Kodak Panatomic X film, ASA Rating 35 (very fine grain), is recommended. It was the film used exclusively in photographing the statues in this book.

The lens stop setting is F16. A small lens opening will give the widest possible range of focus and will assure sharpness in figure's appendages.

The shutter should be set for time exposure. Use shutter-release cable and clock or watch with second hand.

To capture the various subtle tones in garment folds and shadow areas, shoot for a one to two stop overexposure. Fine grain film has the latitude required to tolerate overexposure.

Here, too, it pays to experiment some. You'll find that each statue's finish photographs somewhat differently and each will have its particular requirements for best results. A gold bronze, for example, is highly reflective and needs only a 15-second exposure; an acid, dark brown patina, on the other hand, commands a full minute exposure.

Also bearing on the quality of the end product is the type of paper used for the photo prints. If the finished prints appear to be too harsh, instruct your processor to use a #1 paper; if the prints lack contrast, a #3 paper should be employed.

# Index

*Letter (p) refers
to page number.*

A La Mer 277
Achilles 417
Acquis 693
African 619, 659, 660, 731,
761
Aizelin, E. A. p190
Alerte 174
Alligator 184 185
Alloys p201
Almee 561
Amazon 109 314
Anfrie, C. p190
Animals 327-343
Antoni p190
Anvil 724
Aphrodite (see Venus)
Apocrypha, book of 162
Apollo p67
Apple of Discord 520 522
Arabian 550 552 561 620 662
664 665 758 759
Arm
band 113 264 541 664 675
759 795
bracelet 414 550 552 662
664 687 720, 723, 731,
759, 795, 799
Arrow 466
Art Deco (see Deco)
Art Nouveau (see Nouveau)
Artemis (see Diane)
Artist 235 303
Artist, Un Futur 569 573
Ashtray 217 232 279 336 343
763
Asp 274 731
arm band/bracelet 759 799
Athena 419
Au Claire de la Lune 601
Auririedria V. p190
Aurora 300
Austria p206
Autumn 636
Ax in hand 295 378
Aztec 641

Babies, decorative 235 236
447
Bahnert, R. p190
Bacchante 121 151 221 345
349 475 479 491 495 502
597 612
Bacchus 651 653 655
Bacchus, baby 239 399 658
Badminton 617
Banner in hand 295 769
Barbedienne, F. 162 p33 183
185 218 398 485 499 521
528 679
Barde 542
Barrias, L. E. p190
Bartlet, E. p190
Barwig, F. p190
Barye, A. L. p190
Bases p96

Baskets
in hand 319 320 251 398
448 650
on figure 116 786
on base 461 462
decorative 779 780
Bathing attire 277 279 282
286
Beards 292-295 396 388 425
427 521
Beatrice 242
Beck, P. O. p190
Bed 599
Beers, Jan Van p79
Bell 622
Belleuse (see Carrier)
Bergman p190
Berlin 314
Bernardin 648
Berneaux p189
Bernhardt, Sara 582
Besserdigi p190
Bethulia 162
Beyard de la Vingtrie (see
Vingtrie)
Birds
on basket 779 780
on bowl 218
on planter 190 338
in hand 442 444
in nest 441 452 457
on base 441 436 438
on shoulder 439 447 772
Blacksmith 724
Bofill, A. 190
Bologne, J. 190
Bonheur, M. R. 190
Book,
decorative 178 404 513 592
in hand 256 468 646
Bookend 224 290 291 789
790
Bo Peep, Little 431-434
Bosio, F. J. p190
Bouquet 128 130 251 438 508
629 634 648 701 747 793
Bouguereau, W. 357
Bouret, E. p190
Bourgeois, C. A. p190
Bow
on back 172 174 323
on base 508 517
in hand 507 509 510 545
547
Box 257 354 739
Boys p86 397-411 545 555
Braids 206 396 466 545 581
742 797
Brass p201
Breuer, P. p190
Bronzed p200
Brose, C. p190
Brother/sister (group) 125 253
648
Brousse (see Faure)
Brutt, A. K. J. p190
Buffalo 335
Buice p190
Bust
miniature 123 125 126
372-374 380 381 384
563 564 576 577 776
with arms 457 460 561

Bustle 100 376 431
Butterfly 156 299 357 463
604 742
Buzzer, servant 319 230

Cadet, C. (see Causse)
Caduceus 505 719
Caire, Le 581
Callot, J. p190
Candelabre 183 184 778
Candle stick 592 601 775
Canteen, gourde 399 624 656
522 573
Card dish 239
Carlier, E. J. N. p190
Carrier-Belleuse, A. E. p190
Cartier, T. F. p190
Castenettes 523 537 594
Cat 464 714
Causse, C. p190
Cavalier 292 293 425 427 596
Celia 304
Cello 547
Ceribelli, C. p190
Chalk p62
Charity 197
Charmeur de Serpents 731
Chartier, Alain 692
Charron, A. J. p190
Chemillier, G. de p190
Cheret, J. G. p190
Cherub 186 447 512 768 787
Chien du St. Bernard 644
Children, workers 131 180 251
407 622 624 659
Classical style 206 262 799
Clodion, C. M. p190
Clover, four-leaf 249 556
Clown 222 540 604 607
Cock 718
Collas, A. 162 p33
Colle, A. p190
Collin & Cie. p189
Columbian Exposition p30
Combat 314 326 414 485 602
714
Comic-strip 202 572
Commedia Dell Arte p30
Commissioned piece 197 396
Competition, special p133 569
vs. 573 723 vs. 724
Conquistadores 294 295 425
Copies p200
Copper p201
Copper-plate p202
Copyright 339
Cordier, C. H. J. p190
Corfu 417
Cottin, R. p189
Coudray, M. A. L. p190
Couvre-Feu, Le 622
Crusaders 269
Crystal Palace 314
Culuche, L. p190
Cumberworth, C. 190
Cupid p75
as baby 21,0 364 508 509
512 513
as boy 172 174 507 510
as man 357 517
Curfew 622
Curtz, T. p190
Cymbals 113 349 491 612 655

Dale, C. B. Co. p189
Dalila 301
Date, incised
    1839-499
    1865-528
    1866-581
    1874-318
    1879-162
    1889-720
    1890-148
    1900-170
    1900-326
    1907-629
    1923-539
Dated bronzes p208
David p157 675 679
Debut, M. p190
Debut, J. D. p190
Decauville p189
Deco, Art 136 138 142 149
    231 490 539 757 789
Derniere p190
Deterioration p202
Diane 109 p67 321-323 466
Dionysus (see Bacchus)
Doe 334
Dog p133
    figure 328 332 641 642
    group 337 466 569-573 607
        644 645 732
Domenech Y Vicente p190
D'or, Medaille (see medal)
Drinking
    bowl 152
    chalice 653 597 345 292
    cup 180
    gourde 651
    hand 224
    shell 502
Drouot, E. p190
Drum 214 364 734
Dubois, P. p191
Duboy, P. p191
Duchoiselle p191
Dumaige, E. H. p191
Duret, F. J. p191
Dutrion p191

Eagle 341
Earrings, Hanging 457 581
Eastern figures 269 274
Eichler, T. K. p191
Electroplate 574
Elephant 698 764
Emblem p196
Entre Deux Amours 210
Eros (see Cupid)
Erotic 121 244 246 p136 491
    599
Eusele p191
Exposition 269
    1851-314
    1867-183
    1876-505
    1882-192
    1889-269 693
    1893-105 554
    1898-543
    1900-170 326

Fabrication Francaise p189
Fairy 262 773 775

Fakes p200
Fan 100 720
Falguiere, J. A. J. p191
Fates, three 488 609
Faure de Brousse, V. D. p191
Faust 396 744 749
Fear, expression of 644 648
    649 650 658
Field Co., M. p189
Fencing 414
Ferrand, E. J. p191
Fife 731
Fire-wood 635 649
Fishing 168 289 410 786
Fleur-de-lis 548
Floreal 554 586
Florentine Singer 528
Flower in hand 148 242 248
    249 251 262 299 320 438
    431 451 586 629 634
Flying figures 262 354 357
    719
Fountain 400 697
Fouquet, E. F. p191
Francaise, Fabrication 189
Frederich the Great 645
French bronze p200
Fremiet, E. p191
Friedenau, A. N. p189
Fritzsche, M. p191
Frog 192 445
Fuller Loie 140 766
Fused styling 615 688 787 793

Games of skill 171 181 182
    402 403 423 693 710 756
    757
Gargoyles 183
Garnier, J. p191
Gaudez, A. E. p191
Gautier, G. p191
Geiss p204
Germain, G. B. p191
Get Up! 607
Gibson, Charles Dana 634
Gil Blas 427
Gladenbeck & Sohn 136 148
    150 152 314 406 417 512
    697
Gloves 100 388 389 425 427
Goat 763
Godeau, E. p189
Godet, H. p191
Gold Medal (see Medal)
Goldscheider 191
Goliath p157 679
Goose 485
Gothic 215
Gotz, J. p191
Gounod 396 744 747 749
Goupil & Cie. p189
Grandmother 482
Gregoire, J. L. p191
Grimm's Fairy Tales 445
Grundmann, B. p191
Guillemin, E. C. p191
Guillot, T. A. p191
Guirande, T. D. p191
Gurschner, G. p191
Gypsy 608

Hackstock, K. p191

Hafner p191
Hamburg 401
Harlequin p30 162 164 166
    539
Harp 274 542
Harvest 635 636 637 640 788
Hebrew p157 p162
Heingle, A. p191
Helen of Troy p116
Hennin 459 744
Henry IV, King 382 383
Hepheastus 354
Hera 519
Hercules 398 485 656
Herlinger, T. p191
Hermes (see Mercury)
Hiller, C. J. p191
Hippolyta 109
Holes p202
Holofernes p162
Hoop 154 605 738 756
Horn 304 475 479
    blowing 300 364 512 490
        652
Hors Concours 113 213 277
    441 644 702 733
Horse 314 318 327 330 333
    419
    Trojan 421
Hottot, L. p191
Houdon, J. A. p191
Hubert, R. p191
Hudelet, H. P. p191
Hurdy-Gurdy 536
Huzel p191

Iffland, I. p191
Imitations p200
Improvisateur 170
Incroyable 387 450
Indian 414
Infantry regiment 768
Inkwell 220 222 223 225 229
    335 337 761 782
Iron 193 642 p203
Italian 719 720 733
Ivory 319 320

Jardiniere 188 190
Jew 157 162
Joan of Arc 378 379
Jester 100 668
Jouffrey, F. p191
Judith p162 686 687
Jullien, E. p189
Juno (see Hera)
Jupiter (see Zeus)

Kaesbach, R. p191
Kann, L. p191
Kassin, J. p191
Kauba, C. p191
Keg 644
Kesk, H. p191
Kinsburger, S. p191
Kiss, K. A. E. p191
Kley, L. p192
Knife 326 569 573
Knight, C. R. p192
Knurling 262 601 675 686
Korschann, C. p192
Kruse, B. F. E. p192

L'Age D'or 634
Lamb 432 433 434 615
Lamp 664 665 764 774
    base 192 400 433 442 750
      751 793 749
Lafon Mollo p192
Lanceray, I. A. p192
Laoust, A. L. A. p192
LaPorte, E. H. p192
Larche, R. p192
Lavergne, A. J. p192
Leblune 192
Lecornet, N. (Lecorney) p192
Leda 519
Le Diabolo 171
Lemarquier, C. p192
L'Emir 269
Leonard, A. p192
Leopard 314 326 658 761
LeSage 427
Le Trefle 248
LeVasseur, H. L. p192
Leveque, E. L. A. p192
Lillo, R. p192
Limet, P. p211
Lissy Elkart 202
Listed p207
Lointaine, Princess 582
Loiseau Rousseau p192
Longfellow 380
Lormier, E. p192
Louchet p189
Louvre 718
Lucerne 789
Luxembourg Gallery 528
Lys 310

Madonna 213
Magazine of Art p33
Mandolin 113 170 186 306
    holding 701 702 705
    playing 524 528 543 550
      601 749
Marble p96 p203
Marguerite 396 744 747
Marin, J. C. p192
Marioton, E. p192
Mask 162 164 166 200
Masquerade 200
Match 231 331 343
Medals
    2nd Prize
      1851-542
      1904-724
      1906-754
    1st Prize
      1864-718
      1870-679
      1888-241
      1893-274
    Honorable Mention
      1893-411
      1904-723
    Medal of Honor
      1865-528
      1879-162
    Gold Medal
      1890-299
      1891-656
      1900-326
    Grand Prize
      1899-237

Medicine, patron god 719
Medusa 417
Meissen 541
Mene, P. J. p192
Mengin, P. E. p192
Mercie, M. J. A. p192
Mercury 354 505 718 719
Mestais p192
Mexico 641
Meyerbeer 381
Mignon p165 701 702 705
Milan 720
Miniatures p206
Minstrel 543
Miro, R. p192
Miroir D'eau 789
Miroy Fres. p189
Missing parts 150 233 360 399
    444 461 489 512 616 752
Moigniez, J. p192
Moncel, A. E. p192
Moon 321 322 323 466
Moose 340
More p192
Moreau
    Auguste p192
    Hippolyte p192
    Mathurin p192
Mosque 664 665
Mother-child group 113 201
    206 210 213 286 470 797
Moulin, H. A. J. p192
Moveable bronzes p136 227
    589 664 665
Mozart 545
Munich 202
Musician (also see cymbals and
    tambourine)
    cello 547
    drum 364
    harp 274 542
    vielle 535
    mandolin 306 524 528 543
      550 749
    pipe 304 360 364 731
    triangle 358 361
    violin 545
    zither 735
Musket 318 425 427 664 787

Nam Greb p192
Napoleon 377
Neeb p192
Nesbit, Evelyn (Thaw) 634
Nest 441 452 457
Net 289 786
Nouveau, Art
    ladies 140 219 221 547 582
      584 586 587 590 592
    inkwell 220 223 225 229
    ashtray 228 231 238
    bust 310 575 576
    vase 192 237 754
Novak, V. p192
Numbered p209
Nymphe 567

Obituary p33
Occupation 214 216 217 255
    622 624 669
Odysseus 421
O'ge P. M. F. p192

Olympus, Mount p112
Opera 396 668 p165 744 747
    749
    comique 624
Opitz, O. p189
Oracle p112 499-506
Orator 692
Orgie 475
Owl 762

Paix 273 274
Palestine p162
Palette 235 303
Pallez, L. p192
Palm branch 240 542
Pan 502 658
    baby 490 658
Pandiani, A. p192
Pandora 354 739
Panther (see leopard)
Pantomime 601 602
Paperweight 332
Papillon 299
Paris 417 520 522
    judgment p116
Parody 485
Patina p210 p213 p216
Patriotic 690 768
Pax 575
Pedestal 265 396 411 597 613
    742
Peace 240 273 274
Pear 782
Pegasus 384
Pen & ink stand 773
Petermann, J. p189
Peynot, E. p192
Pheasant 343 616
Phryne 105 799
Picault, E. L. p192
Picciole, M. p192
Pierrot 601 602 734
Pig 406
Pillar 454 456 697
Pine cone
    decorative 343 491 495
    in hand 221 349 479 489
Pinedo, E. p189
Piper 214 216 217
Piron, E. D. p192
Pitch-fork 438
Planter 338
Plaque
    title 174 248 269 274 277
      286 434 436 444 p96
      482 542 543 554 693
      702 723 724 756
    wall 758 759
Ple, H. H. p192
Plume hat 542 560 629
    731 735
Porcelain 488
Pornographic 246
Pot metal p201
Potet, L. p192
Pradier, J. J. 193
Premier Bain de Mer 286
Promotion pieces 244 289 570
Prussia 645
Psyche 156 299 p75 357 517
Purse
    male 216 622 646 692 744

223

Quesnel, E. p189
Quiver 174 210 509

Rabbit 329
Raingo Fres. p200
Rake 637
Rallenberg, J. F. p193
Rancoulet, E. p193
Ranieri, A. de p193
Rarity p209
Reduction Mecanique 162 p33
    485 499 528
Reiter, C. p193
Relief, bas 758 759
Resting 438 619 637 662 783
Rigoletto 100 668
Ring in hand 744
Ringel, M. V. p193
Robin Hood 558
Roche, R. p193
Roger, F. p193
Rolando 425
Roses 299 623
Rostand 582
Rousseau (see Loiseau)
Royal Museum 314
Rubin, A. p193
Ruff, A. p193
Rug 227 659 661
Running 718 732
Russian bronzes p67 318 781

Saalmann, E. p193
Sadness 701-705
Sailor 401 756
Saint Marceaux, R. de p193
Saint Petersburg p67
Salmson, J. J. p193
Salon pieces
    1864-718
    1865-528
    1870-679
    1879-162 742
    1882-569 573
    1884-607
    1888-241
    1889-635 636 720
    1893-274
    1896-637
    1898-357
    1902-168
    1903-665
    1904-723 724
    1906-754
    1907-629
    1911-109
Sanson p189
Sapho 305
Satyr
    male 121 193 345 349 491
        505 656 658
    baby 491 495 778 790
    female 246 789
Saul p157
Sautner, F. A. p193
Schaffert p193
Schiller 384
Schoenewerk, A. P. p193
Schwatenberg p193
Scotch 388 389 401
Scotte, T. p193
Seal 122-128 p196
Sectioning p202

Seduction 121 246 349 491
Seifert p193
Seneca 692
Serenade 543
Shepherd 688
Shepherdess p96 431-434 615
Shield
    decorative 733
    in hand 174 417 421
Shy 156 708 771
Signed p205
Silvestre, P. p193
Siot p189
Sisters (group) 116 252 254
    282 448 472 650
Skill (see games)
Slap-stick 164 166 539
Slate 761
Sling 675
Smoking 133 405 407 599 620
Society of Bronzes p62 p79
Soldier 768 781
Somme, T. p193
Sornin, C. F. p193
Soubrette 376
Spaniard 294 295 425 543
Spear in hand 109 417 419
    421 723
Sphinx 244 274 522 609
Staff in hand 431-434 522 616
    646 688
Stag 331 334 342
Stage, base 162 166 249 604
Stein, beer 397
Steiner, C. L. p193
Stock figure 662
Stork 183 766
Straeten, Van Der p79
    366-376 439
Straw hat 133 241 289 410
    452
Stream, crossing 393 432 648
Styx, River 417
Sua, L. p193
Suan, F. p193
Sub-miniature 546 556 557
    563 564 777
Suchetet, A. E. p193
Supha 148 188
Susse (Sussi) p189
Sutton 193
Swan 519
Swimmer 277 279 282 286
Swivel base p96 116 303 387
    432 441 675 768
Sword
    on figure 417 427 542 596
        622 645 646 692
    in hand 240 269 292 318
        382 414 679 686 687
        768
Symbolic Bronze 240 547 640
    690
Syrinx 345 361 495 502

Tahoser 274
Tambourine
    decorative 100 345 491 502
        543 653
    in hand 359 475 479 489
        495 536 552 608
Tam-o-shanter 289 388 389
    401

Tereszczuk p206
Terlinger, H. (also see Her-
    linger) p193
Thermometer 506
Thiebaut p189
Thiermann p193
Tiffany & Co. p189
Tilgner, V. p193
Tillet, P. p193
Titze, A. p193
Toblueigrth p193
Triangle, musical 358 361
Trojan War 417 421 516
Tuch p193
Turtle 778

Undressing 118 153 770
Unsigned p205
Unger, H. p193
Uraeus 274
Urn 186 187 193
Vallet, M. p193
Van Der Straeten p79 366-376
    439
Van De Vin p193
Vase
    Art Nouveau 754
    broken 409
    on base 421 439 522 612
        799
Vasseur (see LeVasseur)
Veiling 687
Venus p75 p116 357 499 508
    509 517 799
Verdi 668
Vicenti (see Domenech)
Victorian p62 393 431 742
Vigil 113
Villanis p62 p193
Vingtrie p193
Violin 545
Vital-Cornu p193
Voltaire 776

Waagen p193
Wagner, G. p193
Wante, E. p193
Warrior 109 269 314 318 675
    679 686 687
Water Babies 192
Water, Fetching 233 400 408
    470 660 661 671 689 697
Wernekinck, S. p193
Werner, K. J. p193
Wheat 636-640 658 788
White metal busts p62
Wiest p189
Winter 635 649
Wreath in hand 138 151 499
    708 773

Yarn 127 263 488 609

Zany in hand 100 479
Zerritsch, F. p189
Zeus 354 519 p116 653
Zielbauer, A. p193
Zinc 314
Zither 735
Zoological 698
Zora 308
Zut! 172